The Gospel Hologram

For Maggie, Antoine, and Hunter

The Gospel Hologram

++++

The Sign on the Cross and the New Testament Gospels

Darek Barefoot

Grandling Valley Press

THE GOSPEL HOLOGRAM

The Sign on the Cross and the
New Testament Gospels

Unless otherwise noted, Scripture quotations are from the
Authorized (King James) Version of the Bible updated for
contemporary English usage and, where sense is affected, by
critical text readings from *Nestle-Aland Novum Testamentum
Graece* (Stuttgart: Deutsche Bibelgesellschaft, 1993).

Quotations in English from the ancient Greek version of the
Hebrew Scriptures, the Septuagint (abbreviated "LXX"), are from
the English translation by Sir Launcelot C. L. Brenton, 1851,
updated for contemporary English usage.

Quotations from the early church fathers are from *Ante-Nicene
Fathers*, A. Roberts and J. Donaldson, eds. (1885), reprinted
(Peabody, MA: Hendrickson 1994).

ISBN   979-8-218-77736-4

Grandling Valley Press
736 Canvasback Circle No. C
Grand Junction, CO 81505

Acknowledgments

My wife, May, has been my steadfast companion and encourager in the production of this book, as in so much else. Without her patient support, which afforded me the opportunity for the research, writing, organizing, and editing, it never would have seen the light of day.

Contents

Introduction

Is the gospel true? After two thousand years of the advancement of human knowledge, are the claims of Christianity worthy of attention, let alone acceptance? Does modern scholarship allow for evidence that the Bible is inspired? Can discussion of spiritual topics be distanced from the culture war rhetoric that so often infects and corrupts it? My ambition is, in what follows, to offer a positive answer to all these questions.

A greater challenge than producing the evidence is persuading many readers that it could exist. Informed observers may question whether there is fresh ground to break in such a well-plowed field. Those less knowledgeable could be so strongly influenced by popular opinion that it is difficult for them to approach the subject objectively. Some Christians become suspicious at the suggestion that they might need or want support for their beliefs beyond what they already know. In fact, believers and unbelievers alike tend to think that "evidence in support of faith" is something of an oxymoron.

Since Christians are often unable to explain, let alone offer reasons for, their belief, it would be tempting to conclude that reasons are irrelevant. Attempts to relate faith to facts are misguided if faith is purely an intuition. On the other hand, perhaps we should not assume too quickly that facts and evidence are incompatible with faith and intuition.

An illustration may help. Think of the human spine. Imagine a young, active person with a healthy backbone, such as a figure skater or a gymnast. Picture the graceful curves of the athlete's back and the suppleness of their upper body as they go through a skating routine or a floor exercise.

Now, think of the spine below its covering of skin and muscle. We might view an x-ray or a preserved human skeleton. In that case, the spine looks less elegant. We see not something smooth and continuous but a series of separate, bony vertebrae linked together. The vertebrae are irregularly shaped, almost jagged. So viewed, the spine is far from beautiful, or at least does not have beauty to compare with an athletic human torso.

Go deeper still, however. Within the harsh, bony exterior of the spine, at its center, is something smooth and continuous. The King James Bible, at Ecclesiastes 12:6, calls it "the silver cord," but we know it as the spinal cord. It is what makes possible the graceful movements of the skater and the gymnast, and it mediates the mysterious phenomenon of bodily sensation.

The Bible may be compared to the spine. The sense Christians have of a dynamic unity among the Scriptures is like the experience of watching an athlete in motion. Intuitively, they believe they hear the Bible speaking to their innermost selves. Readers with a critical eye, whether or not they are believers, see the Bible as a collection of sixty-six ancient books that have, so to speak, the harsh angles and bony projections of vertebrae.

In this book, we'll probe deeply to glimpse the supernaturally smooth cord that unites several key books of the Bible. We will attempt to isolate evidence of the unity of revelation that so impresses believers at an intuitive level.

The book's title requires a word of explanation. A hologram is a virtual three-dimensional image in which the full contours of a represented object are revealed by viewing the image from different angles. Here, I use that word for a literary image in the New Testament gospels consisting of their collective description of the charge fixed over Jesus at the crucifixion, known in tradition by the Latin term *titulus*, or "title." Analysis reveals that the image encodes, on multiple levels, properties of the gospels individually and as a sacred group of documents.

To understand what makes this literary image so remarkable, we'll trace the concept of "gospel" from ancient Judah to the Persian royal court of the late sixth century BCE and then to first-century Jerusalem, Greece, and Rome. We'll learn why some scholars think that the message of the Christian apostle Paul was different from that of Matthew, Mark, Luke, and John. We'll touch on the puzzling question of how those four documents are related to one another.

When we finally reach what I call the gospel hologram, we'll learn how it emerged, was obscured, and came to light again. That leg of our journey will take us from the second-century scriptoriums of Syria and Egypt to the library shelves of the world's oldest monastery, in the Sinai Desert. We'll discover why this literary hologram is so resistant to ordinary explanation and why it points toward other profound intertextual connections that likewise offer glimpses of the silver cord of inspiration.

In the chapters that follow, when I offer dates for events and documents along with other background information, I have tried to stick to what is generally accepted by historians. My goal has been to avoid claims that are historically controversial unless I can extensively support them.

Readers who assume that the books of the New Testament are consistent might wonder why I go to the lengths I do in the first part of the book to demonstrate how closely these writings agree. The credibility of the conclusions that follow requires that, for the sake of argument, we take nothing for granted where early Christianity is concerned and lay our foundation carefully.

How could what amounts to a snippet of information justify so much attention? To make that clear, we must turn our attention to a distant time and an ancient people enthralled with the hope for a better future.

1

A Gospel for Judah

In 540 BCE, a Persian king who had conquered territory as far west as Greece led his army south along the Tigris toward what had been, only a few years before, the richest and most powerful city in the Ancient Near East. The city was Babylon, in what is now southern Iraq. The king was Cyrus the Great. As it turned out, he captured Babylon without serious resistance.[1] Many of the people of the city and the surrounding territory welcomed his victory. A generation earlier, the Babylonians had brought these people to the area by force, removing them far from their homelands. One of these displaced peoples came from Judah in the land of Canaan, or Israel.

What made the Judahites, or Jews, stand out was their devotion to only one God as opposed to the widespread worship of many gods. Just as exceptional was the Jews' idea that this God, Yahweh, while being active within nature, existed somehow apart from it. Audaciously, they thought that this transcendent, invisible, supreme God had groomed them as a special people. They believed that through them God intended, eventually, to bless the entire world and usher in a new

---

1 The story of Babylon's conquest is told in Dan 5:30–31, in the Nabonidus Chronicle 15–16, and in the Cyrus Cylinder 20–24.

kind of nature from which evil, corruption, and even death would be banished.

The Jews believed that because of their unfaithfulness Yahweh had allowed them to be overrun and enslaved by the Babylonians. In Babylon, the sacred writings and traditions of the Jewish captives had sustained them in their national identity, but the prospect of God saving the world through them seemed like an ember of a dying fire. With the conquest of Babylon by Cyrus the Great, Jewish hopes blazed anew. Cyrus had a policy of allowing the repatriation of exiles, and within a short time he issued a decree that permitted Jews to make the long journey back to Israel.

To the Jews, Cyrus's victory and his edict were nothing less than miraculous. God was keeping promises he had once made to restore them to their home country. Not only would God conduct the Jews on their journey, but in the book of Isaiah, chapters 2, 11, 33, 35, 40, 44, and others, he assures them he will revive their monarchy under the royal house of David and meet them in a special way upon their arrival. Here is how Isaiah celebrates the return of the exiles:

> And the ransomed of the LORD shall return, and come to Zion with singing; everlasting joy shall be upon their heads; they shall obtain joy and gladness, and sorrow and sighing shall flee away. (Isaiah 51:11)

Following is the description of God's rendezvous with his people:

> Get you up to a high mountain, O Zion, herald of good tidings; lift up your voice with strength, O Jerusalem, herald of good tidings, lift it up, fear not; say to the cities of Judah, "Behold your God!" Behold, the Lord GOD comes with might, and his arm rules for him; behold, his reward is with him, and his recompense before him. He will feed his flock like a shepherd, he will gather the lambs in his arms, he will carry them in his bosom, and gently lead those that are with young. (Isaiah 40:9–11)

Looked at this way, the grand proclamation of Cyrus concerning the Jews was an expression in part of an even grander proclamation that God was still leading his people toward a glorious future. As that future unfolded, even death would be abolished. "He will swallow up death forever," says Isaiah 25:8, "and the Lord GOD will wipe away tears from all faces."

When the Hebrew of Isaiah 40:9, as well as a similar passage in Isaiah 52:7, was translated into the newly international language of Greek sometime in the second or third century BCE, the heralding of good tidings to Judah was rendered with the word *euangelizo*. This term meant to declare or proclaim a message, especially one that would be welcome to its hearers. A form of the word would later be used in Greek inscriptions from Asia Minor to praise the first of the Roman emperors, Caesar Augustus, for supposedly bringing peace by conquering the ancient world in the first century BCE.[2]

We now have the pre-Christian, Jewish setting for the verb *euangelizo*, "to proclaim good tidings," and the noun *euangelion*, "good tidings" or "good news," which carried over into Latin and via Latin into English as the words "evangelist" and "evangelism." The English synonym "gospel" comes from the Old English words *god spel*, that is, "good speech," good news.

In keeping with the proclamation of Cyrus, large numbers of Jews did return to their homeland. They managed, though with difficulty over many years, to rebuild their capital of Jerusalem and the temple of Yahweh. But God, who had promised to meet them upon their arrival, seemed to miss his appointment or at least was slow to keep it.

Two or three decades after the return from Babylon, the prophet Zechariah assured the people of Judah that God would still visit them in the person of a new king from David's royal house. Just as Solomon, David's son, had come to his coronation riding on a mule, so the Messianic king would come riding on a donkey:

> Rejoice greatly, O daughter of Zion! Shout aloud, O daughter of Jerusalem! Behold, your king comes to you; triumphant and victorious is he, humble and riding on an ass, on a colt, the foal of an ass. (Zechariah 9:9)

---

2   The "good tidings" about Caesar are most famously proclaimed in the Priene Calendar Inscription; see Chapter 4 under the subheading "Marcus Among the Eagles."

The book of Malachi, from the same period, cautioned them that his coming might take them by surprise:

> "Behold, I send my messenger to prepare the way before me, and the Lord whom you seek will suddenly come to his temple." (Malachi 3:1)

What came instead, over the next four and a half centuries, were waves of persecution under the Seleucid Greeks and then political turmoil and conflict within the nation itself. The most holy chamber of Yahweh's temple was violated, first by the Seleucid ruler Antiochus Epiphanes and later by the Roman general Pompey. Under Roman rule, Judea in the late first century BCE was poor, violent, and unstable. Had the good news proclaimed by Isaiah been a mirage?

The Gospel Reborn

From the initial euphoria of the Jews upon returning to their homeland to their despondency under Greek and then Roman domination, we advance another century until we come to the first historical imprint left by Jesus of Nazareth. It consists of the letters of the Christian apostle Paul. You'll notice that we have entirely skipped over the life of Jesus himself. That's because Jesus left no trace in the historical writings we have from the early first century, and the first known records about Jesus are not the four New Testament gospels but Paul's letters.

There are at least two reasons for identifying Paul's letters as the earliest Christian documents. First, these letters are historically situated. The writer of the letters identifies himself as Paul, sometimes with others included as co-correspondents. The recipients are identified, too, most of them consisting of churches in cities of Asia Minor (modern-day Turkey) and Greece. Paul greets people in these churches by name, in some cases.

Besides addressing the specific problems of individual churches and offering general encouragement, Paul writes about his personal history, his travels, his fellow workers, and his dealings with other prominent leaders of the Christian movement, such as James and Peter. Christian writings outside the Bible, such as *1 Clement*, from the late first century, and the *Letter of Polycarp to the Philippians*, from the early second century, refer to Paul and his letters. All of this helps us to put Paul on the map in every sense. It allows us to date his writings to within a decade or so and offers us insight into his circumstances and motives. We cannot do that for other Christian writings of the first century.

The second reason for regarding Paul's letters as the earliest known Christian records is that, while many first- and second-century works cite Paul's letters, Paul's letters do not mention earlier Christian writings. There are a handful of phrases that appear in one or more of the Four Gospels that also appear in Paul's letters, but these are not attributed by Paul to any written sources. One passage, 1 Timothy 5:18, uses the introductory tag, "As the Scripture says," before quoting a verse from the Old Testament book of Leviticus followed by a short phrase found in Luke's Gospel. If the introduction is intended to cover both of the sentences that follow, then here is the first instance of gospel material being called "Scripture," but we can't be certain on that score.

What we are certain of is that the first preserved documents to quote the gospels formally, by their names, were written more than a century after Paul wrote his letters.

Paul's teachings and those of Jesus as presented in the gospels agree on point after point, from doing good to one's enemies to paying taxes to refraining from judging fellow believers. Why, then, wouldn't Paul cite the gospels for support if the gospels were circulating and regarded as inspired records of the very words of Jesus? Apparently, in Paul's day, the gospels had either not yet been written, were not widely distributed, or had not yet been recognized as having the authority of Scripture.

The Four Gospels emerged onto the stage of history gradually over the course of a generation, like travelers coming out of a fog bank. Already we can sense some mystery about them, which we will soon explore more deeply.

Turning again to Paul's letters as our earliest preserved Christian writings, we observe in them the reappearance of the gospel that had gone forth to the Jews returning from Babylon nearly six hundred years before. Paul not only continues that gospel but also enlarges it. In one of his earliest letters, the one to the Galatians, Paul says that the gospel was proclaimed beforehand to Abraham (Gal 3:8). In doing so he endorses the Jewish belief that God had chosen the Israelite people, through their forefather Abraham, as his instrument for blessing the world.

In yet another letter, to the Christians in Rome, Paul says that everyone who believes that Jesus is Lord will be saved (Rom 10:9–13). He goes on to ask how people will believe in Jesus unless someone tells them about him, and then quotes the Greek version of Isaiah 52:7, one of the verses we referenced earlier, which says, in part, "How beautiful are the feet of those who proclaim good news [*euangelizo*]!" (Rom 10:14–15). Paul thereby implies that with the coming of Jesus, God had finally kept his appointment with his people, or, to be precise, God had begun to keep it, since the saving work of Jesus is still unfolding, according to Paul.[3]

To the summary of Paul's gospel in the declaration that "Jesus is Lord," that is, "Jesus is Sovereign," we can add other brief statements gleaned from Paul's letters, such as the following:

> But when the time had fully come, God sent forth his Son, born of woman, born under the law, to redeem those who were under the law, so that we might receive adoption as sons. And because you are sons, God has sent the Spirit of his Son into our hearts, crying, "Abba! Father!" (Galatians 4:4–6)

> For I delivered to you as of first importance what I also received, that Christ died for our sins in accordance with the scriptures, that he was buried, that he was raised on the third day in accordance with the scriptures, and that he appeared to Cephas, then to the twelve. Then he appeared to more than five hundred brethren at one time, most of whom are still alive, though some have fallen asleep. (1 Corinthians 15:3–6)

---

3   Paul's evocation and application of Isaiah's gospel are evident as well in his quotation in Rom 11:26 of Isa 59:20, an announcement of the Redeemer coming to Zion parallel to that of Isa 40:9.

> Paul, a servant of Jesus Christ, called to be an apostle, set apart for the gospel of God which he promised beforehand through his prophets in the holy scriptures, the gospel concerning his Son, who was descended from David according to the flesh and designated Son of God in power according to the Spirit of holiness by his resurrection from the dead, Jesus Christ our Lord. (Romans 1:1–4)

> ...on that day when, according to my gospel, God judges the secrets of people by Christ Jesus. (Romans 2:16)

> For Christ must reign until he has put all his enemies under his feet. The last enemy to be destroyed is death. (1 Corinthians 15:26)

Those are some of the key elements of Paul's gospel: that Jesus is sovereign, that he will one day judge the world, and that his kingdom will bring about the death of death. We can gather that Paul believed Jesus once lived as a real flesh-and-blood man, a Jew, and that he died to remove the effects of sin and afterward rose from the dead.

What Does Paul Say About Jesus?

Because Paul wrote to believers, offering exhortation and addressing problems, his letters don't contain much information about Jesus' earthly life. What can we glean from them in that regard? Paul says in his letter to the Romans that Jesus had ministered primarily to "the circumcision," that is, to Jews, and he says in Galatians that Jesus had a brother named James who was one of the leaders of the Jerusalem church, which implies that Jesus had lived in the Jewish homeland (Rom 15:8; Gal 1:18–19). Paul mentions Jesus' core group of disciples, the apostles, and names Peter and John as being among them (Gal 1:17; 2:9). The book of Ephesians says that Jesus had preached a message of peace and reconciliation with God (Eph 2:17).

In different places Paul's letters say that Jesus had been killed by the world's rulers, which included the Roman Caesar and his appointees, as well as by the Jews, implying that both Jewish leaders and Roman officials were involved in condemning Jesus to crucifixion (1 Cor 2:8; 1

Thess 2:14–15). Paul claims that Jesus had been "betrayed" or "handed over" on the night before his death—exactly how, Paul doesn't say—and that he had shared a communion meal with his disciples (1 Cor 11:23–25).

1 Timothy says that Jesus gave a testimony before Pontius Pilate, the Roman governor of Judea for several years early in the common era, which provides a rough chronological marker (1 Tim 6:13). Academic scholars generally doubt that Paul was the author of some of the books bearing his name, including the letters to Timothy. The question of authorship has little bearing on our purpose here. All the Pauline letters are relatively early Christian documents that circulated within the Christian community of Southern Europe and Asia Minor, and they reflect early preaching about Jesus.

From Paul's letters, we can learn some basic facts about the life of Jesus, but few of the details. There is no mention of exorcisms, healings, or other miracles. There are no quoted sermons or parables of Jesus. And, as I've noted, there is also no mention of documents readers can consult for such information. Did early Christians not need or care to know more about the man whom Paul proclaimed as God's Son?

Let's return to the passage Paul quoted from Isaiah, "How beautiful are the feet of those who proclaim good news!" It was appropriate to a message carried by missionaries like Paul, who traveled on foot to the far reaches of the Roman Empire. The gospel was spread primarily by word-of-mouth, not by documents.

Recall that Paul wrote about Jesus' brother James still living in Jerusalem along with members of Jesus' inner circle of disciples, including Peter and John. There were other witnesses as well. In the middle of the first century, people still living could claim to have personal knowledge of Jesus' life, ministry, death, and resurrection. The stories they told must have circulated by word-of-mouth, the same way Paul preached the gospel. Believers did not have to memorize all these stories; knowing that witnesses to the important facts were still alive was probably enough.

Recording the Testimony

By the late first century, the living witnesses to Jesus were dwindling. Christians in a position to preserve the details of his life must have felt a growing need to do so. Even if the life stories of Jesus were written early, before the middle of the first century, their value would only have become apparent some years later, near the century's end.

The oldest references we have to any of the documents by name are from a Christian named Papias of Hieropolis, whose life straddled the first and second centuries CE. Most of his writings have been lost to history, but a few fragments are preserved in the work of the fourth-century Christian historian Eusebius of Caesarea. In one of these quotations, Papias says that Mark was the interpreter of Peter and that he wrote down what Peter had told him about the sayings and deeds of Jesus.[4]

Papias says that Mark was careful to record information accurately. He further says that Mark did not write down these anecdotes in exact order because Peter had not intended to provide a regular narrative. In other words, Papias implies that Mark had to stitch the remembered stories together, a claim that accords with the vague chronological transitions that we find in the middle portion of Mark's Gospel.

Eusebius goes on to quote Papias as saying that the apostle Matthew assembled the "oracles," meaning sayings by or concerning Jesus, in the Hebrew dialect and that each one interpreted them as best he could. Did Papias mean that Gentile readers had to translate these sayings for themselves? Perhaps he meant that the teachings of Jesus were being preserved in Greek based on sayings and anecdotes originally written by Matthew in either Hebrew or a Hebrew dialect of Aramaic. We can't say for sure.

Papias's comments are respectful of these writings, but not reverential. He says they contain *logia* (scriptural sayings), but he does not refer to them as "Scripture." He talks about Mark's account before that of Matthew, unlike the traditional order of the gospels. Papias fails to men-

---

4   Eusebius, *Ecclesiastical History* III, 39.

tion Luke and John, which most scholars believe to be the last two canonical gospels to be written, although his listing of apostles does follow the order of their appearance in John's Gospel.

Another excerpt reveals Papias's attitude toward the written stories about Jesus. According to Eusebius, Papias claimed that he sought out Christians who had actually known apostles such as Andrew, Peter, Philip, and Thomas and questioned them. He did this, he says, because he valued the living voices that still remained above "what could be got from books."[5] And yet, we have credible testimony from Irenaeus and Eusebius that Papias himself wrote a collection of the sayings of Jesus, which long ago was lost.

Papias not only is the first to directly mention what we now call the gospels, he also gives us a fleeting look at the transition in the second century from oral accounts of Jesus to writings about him. Two other documents from around the time of Papias, the *Epistle of Barnabas* and *2 Clement,* each contain one passage where gospel material is designated as Scripture.[6]

Yet another document possibly from this period, the *Apology of Aristides,* says that Jesus was born of a virgin, as can be read in the gospel, or that one can learn such things about him from the gospel writing (versions of the book vary on this point).[7]

Within perhaps twenty years of Papias, Justin Martyr would refer to the gospels as the "memoirs of the apostles." Justin doesn't say how many books he is referring to or name the authors. He does allude to a passage from Mark's Gospel and says it is from the memoirs of Peter, who, as we just saw, was the source of Mark's information according to Papias. Justin is our earliest witness to the use of the word *euangelia,* "gospels," to describe written stories of Jesus' life.[8]

---

5   Loc. cit.
6   *2 Clement* 2:4 (cf. Mark 2:17; Matt 9:13); *Epistle of Barnabas* 4:14 (cf. Matt 22:14).
7   The *Apology of Aristides,* chapter 2 (Syriac version), chapter 15 (reconstructed Greek version).
8   *First Apology of Justin Martyr* 66.3.

Apparently, the existence of multiple accounts of Jesus' life troubled Justin's pupil Tatian, who nevertheless recognized that four of them were too popular to ignore. He tried to solve the problem by blending them into a single narrative that came to be called the *Diatessaron*, meaning "through the four." The *Diatessaron* was well-known in Syria, but it never replaced the four primary sources from which it was created. Irenaeus, who was roughly contemporary with Tatian, offers us our first clear description of the gospels under their names and accords them the fully sacred status that Christians have ever since.

Will the Real Evangelists Please Stand Up?

When a person appears as a witness in a court of law, the first testimony he or she must give is their name. The person describes what they saw and heard and how they were able to see and hear it. The more serious the issue, more vital it is to know the identity of the witnesses and the circumstances bearing on their testimony.

Now consider the twenty-seven documents of the New Testament. They are referred to as books, but the majority are letters or circulars in letter form. With the exception of the Letter to the Hebrews and the three small books of John, the New Testament letters contain an identification of the writer or writers within the text, most often Paul. A letter intended for a specific recipient or group was typically entrusted to a courier who was often a friend of both the writer and addressees (Eph 6:21–22), in which case the courier could, at least in theory, vouch for the letter's origin.

Of the New Testament books that are not letters, five are either life stories of Jesus or, in the case of the book of Acts, a historical supplement to such an account. Revelation is the only book that is neither a letter nor appended to a Jesus story. In the text of that book, the writer identifies himself four times, at 1:1, 1:4, 1:9, and 22:8. In the last of these, the writer says, "I John am he who heard and saw these things." The writer also heightens his claim of eyewitness testimony by narrating Revelation in the first person.

The Evangelists could have named themselves within the texts of the gospels, but none of them does. The closest any comes to doing so is in John 21:24, which says, "This is the disciple who is bearing witness to these things, and who has written these things; and we know that his testimony is true." Who is "this disciple"? Earlier he is called "the disciple whom Jesus loved," who was with Peter on the shore of Galilee. Tradition says that it was John the son of Zebedee, but John's Gospel never explicitly reveals the name of the beloved disciple. The verse refers to him in the third person while speaking in the first person plural "we," suggesting that an editor has added a note to an earlier record.

Some scholars point out that in Greco-Roman biographies of Late Antiquity, often the author's name was not contained in the text. Christian discourse of the time, however, carried a particular concern for such disclosure.

Both John the son of Zebedee and Matthew are listed as apostles of Jesus (Matt 10:1–2). Their status as eyewitnesses would lend credibility and authority to what they wrote (Acts 13:31). Even if they did not identify themselves directly, they could have stated how they knew about the events they recorded. Having firsthand knowledge would have qualifed them to write in the first person, as did John of Patmos in the book of Revelation. The New Testament itself confirms that the identities of witnesses and teachers are important. For example, in Acts 24:18–19, Paul says that those bringing accusations against him should show themselves in public to make their charges.

In 2 Timothy 3:14, the recipient of the letter is reminded that he believes what he does in part because of knowing the identities and character of those who taught him. The writer of the letter of 2 Peter both identifies himself as Simon Peter the apostle and asserts his standing as an eyewitness of the transfiguration of Jesus during his ministry (2 Pet 1:16–18). We would expect to find the same combination of self-identification and professed eyewitness status in the Gospels of Matthew and John if they were written directly by apostles.

The author of Luke makes no pretense of being an eyewitness. He says in his introduction that other accounts of Jesus had already been written (though he declines to name them), and that the sources of generally accepted information about Jesus include eyewitnesses, none of whom he actually claims to have interviewed.

The gospels do have titles bearing the purported names of the authors. The full titles are "The Gospel (*tou euangelion*) According to Matthew," "...Mark," "...Luke," and "...John." It would be odd, to say the least, for the four Evangelists to have independently chosen identical formats for their titles. Did the first of them create the wording, and then the others imitate it?

Imagine the first gospel writer sitting down with blank papyrus or preparing to dictate to a scribe. He is about to tell the story of the greatest man who ever lived, the Savior of the World, the Lord of the Universe, and the only Son of the Almighty God, but instead of writing "Jesus of Nazareth" at the top of the page, he writes...his own name? It would be less appropriate for the author to name himself in the title than to do so in the body of the document, as John does in Revelation. The titles must have been given to the accounts about Jesus sometime after they were written, as happened with the New Testament letters.

How, then, should we treat the question of who wrote the gospels? The absence of internal authorship claims does not exclude inspiration or the status of the documents as divine revelation. Whether or not the names attached to the gospels are those of the actual writers, those names nevertheless are appropriate in memorializing the earliest disciples and their companions, who must necessarily be the individuals responsible for transmitting whatever historical information the gospels contain.

It is unclear why the Evangelists chose not to include more information about themselves in their works. Each of the gospels therefore comes with a bit of mystery attached. In its own way, each combines realistic details about time and place with narrative artistry. Each Evangelist tells a story tightly focused on Jesus, then invites us to make of it what we will.

The secrecy of the Evangelists about their identities is not the only puzzling question we will encounter on our journey toward the gospel hologram. But the next one is easier to answer.

2

Narratives Become Gospels

The next question concerning ancient accounts of Jesus' life is why they were labeled "gospels." As we have seen, "the gospel" originally referred—and continues to refer—to the general message of salvation through Jesus preached by missionaries. The New Testament has a synonym for *euangelion*, "gospel," and that word is *kerygma*, "preaching" or "proclamation."

The first four books of the New Testament are long, written narratives. The gospel message of salvation, by contrast, is a brief, powerful statement or short series of statements delivered by a preacher, along with an invitation to believe. They would seem to be different forms of information. For example, two of the life stories of Jesus, Matthew and Luke, contain nativities that inform us about Jesus' birth. We find no birth stories in Paul's gospel. Those same two documents contain genealogies of Jesus; no genealogies are found in Paul's writings.

The life stories relate acts of healing, exorcism, and power over nature, whereas Paul describes no miracles of Jesus except his resurrection. Jesus teaches in sermons, parables, and prophecies in the written narratives, but Paul quotes no sermons or parables of Jesus as part of his gospel.

How, therefore, did the life stories come to be called "gospels"? An explanation advanced by some scholars is that the designation "gospels"

was applied to the life stories of Jesus in error.[9] According to this explanation, the shift in the meaning of the word occurred in the middle 140s
of the second century, when an apostate Christian teacher named Marcion of Sinope gained a following.

Marcion did not believe that the God of the Hebrews, Yahweh, was
the Father of Jesus or that the Hebrew Bible has spiritual value. Marcion accepted certain letters of Paul because they emphasize faith
rather than adherence to the Law of Moses. Perhaps because of Luke's
association with Paul, Marcion also accepted Luke's story of the life of
Jesus, although apparently Marcion felt the need to excise portions of
Luke that drew heavily on the Scriptures of Israel.

Marcion, it seems, thought that where Paul in his letters speaks of
"my gospel" or "our gospel" (e.g., Rom. 2:16), he is referring to Luke's
narrative about Jesus.[10] The speculation is that because Marcion valued
writings above oral traditions, which he thought were corrupted by Judaism, he believed that Paul must have learned the gospel from a document, namely, Luke's story of Jesus' life. In responding to Marcion,
Justin Martyr and other orthodox teachers unwittingly adopted his mis-
taken definition of "gospel." Before long, all the Jesus narratives were
given titles that reflected this new usage.

The theory of Marcion's infectious error, though it fits some key facts,
has a weakness. Marcion thought that Christian writings could only be
trusted after he himself had reconstructed them. It is unclear why, in
Marcion's belief system, Luke's story of Jesus remained untainted until
Paul learned the gospel from it. If God delivered a pure document about
Jesus into Paul's hands, he might just as easily have made sure that Paul
heard pure oral teaching. Marcion and his followers spread their message in part by verbal preaching.

Marcion's curious version of church history by itself does not explain
why he would suddenly confuse the message of salvation with a written
narrative about Jesus, inasmuch as Christians until then had naturally
distinguished between them. Marcion's mistake is easier to understand

---

9   Helmut Koester, *Ancient Christian Gospels*, 35–37.
10 Tertullian, *Against Marcion*, IV.2–4.

as the result of a new, expanded use of the word "gospel" than as its cause. In all likelihood it was because the word "gospel" had begun to be applied to the life stories of Jesus that Marcion clumsily misunderstood Paul's language.

If Marcion did not introduce the new definition of "gospel," where did it come from? One of the first places to look is in the introduction to Mark's account of Jesus. Papias, as we have noted, first names the Evangelists, and the first one he mentions is Mark. Here is how Mark begins:

> The beginning of the gospel of Jesus Christ, the Son of God. As it is written in Isaiah the prophet, "Behold, I send my messenger before your face, who shall prepare your way; the voice of one crying in the wilderness: 'Prepare the way of the Lord, make his paths straight.'" (Mark 1:1–3)

Might the introductory line have been intended as the title of the story that follows? "The beginning of the gospel of Jesus Christ, the Son of God" is not a sentence, but it is awkwardly long for a title, even if the ending words, "the Son of God," are not included. Nevertheless, a scribe might well look at this string of words to create a title. The Hebrew titles of several books of the Old Testament, including those we know as Genesis, Exodus, Leviticus, Numbers, and Deuteronomy, incorporate words taken from the opening phrases of those books.

Naming the Narratives

Think again about the book of Revelation, or Apocalypse, the only book outside the Jesus life histories and Acts that is not a letter. How did it acquire the title it has in the earliest manuscripts, which is "A Revelation of John"? The book opens as follows:

> The revelation of Jesus Christ, which God gave him to show to his servants what must soon take place; and he made it known by sending his angel to his servant John. (Revelation 1:1)

As in Mark, the first line is a long introductory fragment. The most prominent word in that introduction is *apokalypsis*, "revelation," a word that occurs elsewhere in the New Testament with a range of meanings. The *Apocalypse of Baruch* and the *Apocalypse of Peter* were other early books of this genre, so "Revelation" could not stand by itself for long. The way the title of Revelation is related to its introduction is a close parallel to the way the word "gospel" is related to the introduction of the narrative ascribed to Mark.

Suppose a scribe preparing a collected edition of the gospels had a history of Jesus in which Peter is the foremost disciple. The lack of a resurrection appearance was inconsistent with authorship by Peter (1 Cor 15:5). The scribe had a letter reputedly from Peter that lists Mark as Peter's companion, however (1 Pet 5:13). The scribe had another Jesus story that, curiously, uses the apostolic name "Matthew" of a tax collector whom the first document calls by the seemingly non-apostolic name "Levi" (Matt 9:9; Mark 2:14; cf. 3:16–19). A third such document came to light, whose author is associated with the circle of Paul the Apostle by its companion volume, Acts. Paul's last known companion is named as Luke in 2 Timothy 4:11.

Finally, our scribe had in his collection a gospel known to have begun circulating when only one of the key church pillars named by Paul could still have been living, namely, John (Gal 2:9). The shortest of these four documents might well have supplied a template for giving titles to the others. It could have been the first such account the scribe was familiar with, but in any case, its opening was more suggestive of a title than were those of the other narratives.

A scribe who noticed Mark's initial emphasis on the word "gospel" would see its appropriateness as a title confirmed by the author's introductory voice. Unlike Matthew, Luke, or John, Mark's opening has a tone of announcement or declaration that fits the concept of gospel in the Greek version of Isaiah.

Mark almost immediately quotes from Isaiah 40, concerning the prospect of God meeting the people of Judah after they returned from their exile. "Prepare the way for the Lord," in Isaiah 40:3, leads into verse 9, which we read back in Chapter 1. Verse 9 is where the herald of glad tidings is told to announce to the cities of Judah, "Behold, your God!" Mark conveys the same message as Paul had when Paul quoted a parallel passage from Isaiah 52. In Jesus, God had kept—and was keeping—his appointment with Israel.

Mark's opening, therefore, has an emphatic occurrence of the word "gospel," a tone of proclamation, and a quotation from the original gospel to Judah. "Gospel" could not stand by itself in the title because of other documents of the same kind, just as "Revelation" could not in the Revelation of John. Whatever the process by which it was assigned, the title given to Mark fit admirably and was adapted to the other three narratives of Jesus' life.[11]

The plural form of the word used by Justin Martyr, "gospels," is also easy to explain. The form of the title in ancient manuscripts is not the Gospel "of" Mark or Matthew, as if the reports were fundamentally different, but the Gospel "according to" Mark, Matthew, and Luke, indicating different versions of the same essential story. Habits of speech are such that speakers lapse into plurals through abbreviation. Today we might refer to "Bibles" when we mean different translations of the Bible, such as the King James Version or New International Version.

Similarly, although Paul did refer to "my gospel" in Romans and "the gospel of the uncircumcision" and "of the circumcision" in Galatians, a careful reading of his statements as a whole shows that he believed in one gospel message that might be delivered with a different emphasis depending on the audience (Gal 2:2, 7).

We now have an idea of how the Jesus narratives might have come to be called gospels. We've also demonstrated that what Paul preached and what Mark wrote had in common the message that, in Jesus, God had kept his appointment with his people.

Nevertheless, there still seems to be a gulf between Paul and the Evangelists. Paul preached, "Believe that Jesus is Lord and be saved." Mark, Matthew, Luke, and John invited readers to sit down and learn what Jesus did, what he said, where he went, who believed and followed him, and who opposed him. We still have those two categories:

11　Scholars tend to class the New Testament gospels with ancient biographies, but the gospels depart importantly from what is usually defined by the English language word "biography." I have, therefore, opted to use the more general terms "narrative," "life history," and "life story."

(1) the gospel message of salvation and (2) the remembrances about Jesus. Though they concern the same person, Jesus of Nazareth, they seem to be different types of information.

As we just said, Paul preached, "Believe that Jesus is Lord and be saved." "Jesus is Lord" can be paraphrased as "Jesus is sovereign, worthy of all honor, obedience, and reverence." Paul also repeatedly refers to faith in "Jesus Christ," which requires belief that Jesus is Christ. Christ, or *Christos*, is the Greek equivalent of the Hebrew *Mashiach*, the Messiah, the Anointed.

When a king was crowned or a high priest was installed in Israel, perfumed oil was poured over his head as a symbol of God's Spirit coming down over and into him to imbue him with power and wisdom. The gospel proclamation of Isaiah and Zechariah was that God would meet his people in the person of an anointed king of the house of David.

Jesus himself had come preaching the gospel, saying, "Repent, for the kingdom of God is at hand," according to Matthew 4:17. Jesus thereby announced that God was keeping his long-awaited appointment with his people. Jesus preached and taught without using the traditional formula "Thus saith the Lord" or by citing the names of rabbis with whom he agreed or disagreed. Jesus said, "I say to you," as if he had God's own authority. He commanded people to follow him, trust him, and forsake all else for him. Jesus, in other words, presented himself as Lord and Sovereign over the lives of human beings.

Jesus also claimed to be the unique Son of God by speaking as if God were, in a direct sense, his Father. He did not announce himself as the Messiah, but by referring to himself as the future judge of the world, he invited his listeners to conclude that he was, indeed, the long-promised anointed king. He did not preach openly that he would die for the world's sins, but from the beginning of his ministry, he faced the murderous hatred of his adversaries to offer forgiveness, healing, and spiritual knowledge to those who came to him. He preached self-sacrifice as the path to exaltation and that a person must lose their life to find it.

What Paul declared about Jesus coincided with what Jesus' own preaching would have implied to his hearers. Moreover, Paul's gospel expands in scope as we provide the background necessary to understand such titles as Lord, Son of God, and Christ in terms of God's promises to Israel.

Paul doesn't just assign Jesus titles, of course. Earlier we learned that Paul taught that Jesus came as a flesh-and-blood man, not a phantom. That was from Galatians 4. Here it is again:

> But when the time had fully come, God sent forth his Son, born of woman, born under the law, to redeem those who were under the law. (Galatians 4:4)

These words, made more forceful by their rhythm, amount to a miniature nativity story—a birth narrative, though a brief one. The nativities of Matthew and Luke are longer, more detailed versions. Luke even shows dramatically that Jesus was "born under the law [of Moses]" by relating that Jesus was circumcised and taken to the temple as an infant. It is inaccurate, therefore, to claim that Matthew and Luke have nativity stories and Paul's writings do not. Paul's nativity is simply short and undetailed.

Paul Documents Jesus

I can drive through the same city streets for years and fail to see parts of the landscape. Then I'll suddenly realize that a certain house has an odd architectural feature or that a small cafe is tucked away in an office complex. It's possible, too, to read the letters of Paul and not realize that he has a small, spare nativity story in the fourth chapter of Galatians.

What about another claim, that Paul provides no genealogy of Jesus, as do Matthew and Luke? Here is Paul again: "The gospel concerning his [God's] Son, who was descended from David according to the flesh" (Rom 1:3).

Matthew and Luke trace Jesus' lineage to before David but highlight him because the Messiah, the *Christos*, was expected to be his descendant. In Romans 1:3, quoted above, Paul provides an abbreviated genealogy, just as he does an abbreviated nativity in Galatians. Jesus, we learn, was from the family line of David.

That Jesus had Davidic ancestry is repeated in 2 Timothy and Revelation.[12] In the book of Acts, Peter tells Jews in Jerusalem that Jesus was from David's family without going into detail about Jesus' birth. Paul does the same in Romans 1:3. Paul had some knowledge of Jesus' family because he had met one of Jesus' brothers, James, in Jerusalem (Gal 1:19). Paul doesn't feel the need to elaborate; he writes as if Jesus' family descent from David was generally acknowledged. How could such a claim be accepted so easily?

In the ancient world, people were less mobile than they are today. Most people lived and died in the village or city where they were born. This was even more the case among Jews in Palestine. Jewish law made it difficult to sell family property. Purchase of ancestral land was more like a lease, with the land reverting to the original family owners after a certain number of years.

The law of ancestral possession is found in the book of Leviticus, chapter 25, verses 23–28. Even if that law was not strictly observed, it indicates that there was a cultural premium on retaining possession of ancestral properties and social pressure on purchasers of such properties to allow redemption by the family of original ownership. In 1 Kings 21:3, the king of Israel offers to buy the vineyard of one of his subjects, and the man replies, "The LORD forbid that I should give you the inheritance of my fathers."

Partly as a result of the cultural value placed on familial property, families remained anchored to the same locale generation after generation. Even when peasant farmers moved away to escape economic hardship, the ancestral plot might draw them back years later. Repatriation and reclamation of family land is the historical backdrop of the Old Testament book of Ruth. As Ruth illustrates, people in rural towns or villages tended to be related to one another because of intermarriage over time within the same limited population.

Whatever records or memories a person might claim to have to prove their ancestry, knowledge of where that person's relatives lived was perhaps the best evidence. The easiest way to credibly claim a fam-

---

12   2 Tim 2:8; Rev 5:5; 22:16.

ily relationship with David would be to have relatives of long-standing in Bethlehem, the village where David reputedly was born and had ancestral land. John's Gospel emphasizes this connection. In debating about Jesus, Jewish observers are quoted as asking, "Has not the scripture said that the Christ is descended from David and comes from Bethlehem, the village where David was?" (John 7:42). Ancestry and village went together.

For Paul to be able to say, without argument or detail, that Jesus was of the line of David probably means that Jesus was known to have relatives in Bethlehem, the town of David. Paul never mentions Nazareth as the town where Jesus grew up, but early Christians are unlikely to have invented that information. If Jesus' legal father was a builder, as the gospels say, then he may have originally moved from Judea to Galilee because work was available in the larger city of Sepphoris near Nazareth.

Jesus having relatives in both Bethlehem and Nazareth is, therefore, credible apart from Matthew's and Luke's nativity stories. That in turn lends a degree of support to the idea that Jesus was somehow born in Bethlehem but raised in Nazareth. Therefore, although Paul does not relate the circumstances of Jesus' birth, the information he does provide is consistent with the birth accounts in the gospel canon.

What about the claim that Jesus was born to a virgin? Paul does not refer to a virginal conception in the womb of Mary, but he does say that Jesus was of David's family "according to the flesh" in Romans 1:3. He uses a similar phrase in Romans 9:5. Paul says "according to the flesh" because elsewhere he claims that Jesus was God's own unique Son, as we can see, for example, in Romans 8:3, 32. Paul presents us with the profound union of fleshly human nature and divine nature in Jesus that suggests a conception at once supernatural and, somehow, human.

Paul and the Ministry of Jesus

As we've seen, Paul informs his readers about Jesus as a flesh-and-blood man in first-century Palestine. What can we learn from Paul about Jesus as a rabbi and healer?

Paul confirms that Jesus had a ministry and that it was directed primarily toward the Jews (Rom 15:8). He suggests that Jesus performed healings and other powerful works, though he relates no miracle stories.

In 2 Corinthians 5:20, Paul explains that he is preaching in the stead of Jesus himself. He says that he is an imitator of Jesus at 1 Corinthians 11:1. He says that Christ was revealed through him in Galatians 1:16. If Paul was following Jesus' example, then Jesus must have worked miracles to confirm his message. Paul says the following:

> For I will not venture to speak of anything except what Christ has wrought through me to win obedience from the Gentiles, by word and deed, by the power of signs and wonders, by the power of the Holy Spirit, so that from Jerusalem and as far round as Illyricum I have fully preached the gospel of Christ. (Romans 15:18–19)

The same combined Greek terms for "word and deed" and "signs and wonders" here used by Paul likewise occur in descriptions of the miracles of Jesus (Luke 24:19; John 4:48; Acts 2:22).

What was true of Paul was true of the first-century church as a whole. Paul likens the church to Christ's body, his collective earthly agent, in 1 Corinthians 12, in the very place where he speaks about the modes of ministry of the church, such as the offices of apostles, prophets, and teachers, and gifts of healings, tongues, interpretations, and miracles (1 Cor 12:1–31). Paul reminds the Galatians that "he who works miracles among you" does so by virtue of their faith rather than because of merit under the Law of Moses (Gal 3:5); this implies that Jesus had worked miracles among his followers and that these were closely tied to faith, which is in fact what we find in the Four Gospels.[13]

A miracle present in the early church but not in Jesus's ministry is that of speaking in "tongues," that is, in languages not learned but rather ecstatically experienced. We can find a connection in 1 Corinthians 14:2, however, where Paul refers to such expressions as *mysteria*, "mysteries," because they could not be readily understood by hearers. Ecstatic speech is grouped with inspired revelation, prophecy, and inter-

---

13 E.g., Matt 9:2; 17:19–20; Mark 10:52; Luke 7:50; John 14:12; cf. Acts 14:9.

pretation (1 Cor 14:5–6, 26). The stories about Jesus make clear that he, too, had spoken under inspiration.

Onlookers were astonished at Jesus' teaching and remarked that no man had spoken like him (Mark 1:22; John 7:46). Although in the gospels Jesus does not speak in unlearned tongues, he does speak in parables and figures not readily understood by the crowd. Jesus interprets his figurative language for the disciples, as portrayed in Mark 4:1–23. The obscure sayings of Jesus, like utterances in tongues, are called *mysteria* (Matt 13:11). Jesus' ministry had elements similar to the inspired speech of revelation and prophecy of the early church, including strange expressions requiring interpretation.

Speaking of parables as such, a frequently occurring parable in the Four Gospels is of a master who entrusts his servants with resources and responsibilities and then goes away in expectation of an accounting upon his return (Matt 24:45–51; 25:14–30; etc.). Paul employs the same image to make the same point about the accountability of individual believers, though not as a full-blown parable (1 Cor 4:1–5; Rom 14:4).

Paul said that he had divine power to overturn anything raised against the knowledge of God (2 Cor 10:3–4), and that his congregations could discern between the Spirit of God and the demonic spirits that led people into idolatry (1 Cor 10:19–21; 12:2–3). These abilities served as manifestations of Jesus' power to expose and defeat dark spiritual forces.

Paul's writings do not depict the scribes and Pharisees confronting Jesus, but Paul does say that by suffering tribulation on behalf of the word of God, Christians in Thessalonica were following the example of the Lord himself, as well as that of Paul and of Jewish Christians (1 Thess 1:6; 2:14). In Romans, Paul alludes to the resistance and persecution Jesus encountered in the course of his ministry by saying that he had suffered reproaches in obedience to God's will (Rom 15:3).

Paul points out that persons who zealously promoted adherence to the Law of Moses could be found to have broken it themselves (Rom 2:17–23). Jesus likewise had charged Jewish religious leaders with hypocrisy insofar as they kept the externals of the law but violated its deeper principles (Matt 23:23). Like Jesus, Paul urges repentance (Rom 2:4).

A eucharistic meal Jesus instituted among his disciples on the night of his arrest is described by Paul using language similar, particularly, to that in the Gospel of Luke (1 Cor 11:23–25; Luke 22:14–20).

Paul says that the Jewish leaders who opposed Jesus eventually killed him, in keeping with their treatment of the prophets (1 Thess 2:15). The gospels similarly put Jesus in the company of martyred prophets, for example, in the parable of the Vineyard and Tenants (Mark 12:1–9; cf. Luke 13:33–34).

Paul refers often to his expectation of the return of Jesus in supernatural power to gather his people. His letters even contain miniature apocalypses that portray dramatic scenes at the end of earthly history.[14] Here, too, Paul's teaching reflects that of Jesus, having in common with the gospels such figures as the blowing of the celestial trumpet, the clouds of heaven as a vehicle, and the Lord coming like a thief in the night. Three of the gospels have their own longer apocalypses, in Matthew 24, Mark 13, and Luke 21, while John has a short one in chapter 5. All the gospels promise a return of the Messianic Son of Man.[15]

In Philippians 2:5–7, Paul famously says that Christ once enjoyed the "form of God," here meaning not an inner nature but an outward appearance, the glory of divinity. But, Paul says, the Son emptied himself by putting aside this outward splendor and so "came to be in the likeness of men." The first chapter of John's Gospel, which refers to God's preexisting Son as the Word and the light of the world, provides a longer account of the incarnation. Instead of saying that the Son "came to be in the likeness of men," John says, "The word became flesh and made his dwelling among us" (1:1–14). Once again, Paul offers us a brief statement that receives a longer treatment in one of the Four Gospels.

---

14 1 Cor 15:51–54; 1 Thess 4:14–17; 5:2–3.

15 E.g., in Matt 7:22; 10:23; Mark 8:38; 13:21–37; 14:61–64; Luke 17:24–25; John 14:3. Some scholars have speculated that the Son of Man whom Jesus said would come in judgment was not Jesus himself. The gospels themselves intend "Son of Man" to be understood as Jesus (Mark 9:12; John 9:35–37; etc.).

Bridging the Gulf

Although Paul does not quote from written sermons of Jesus, he does set forth moral requirements of chastity, honesty, humility, and selflessness that closely mirror the teachings in the gospels. Paul says to forgo vengeance and do good even to enemies, as does Jesus (Rom 12:19–21; cf. Luke 6:35). Paul tells the Corinthians in the first chapter of his second letter to them that he does not, like an ungodly person, "say 'yes' and 'no' at once," meaning that he did not make promises he had no intention of keeping (2 Cor 1:17–18). Jesus, likewise, in the Sermon on the Mount, says to let your "yes" really mean yes and your "no" mean no (Matt 5:37).

Paul directly cites the command of Jesus regarding the sanctity of marriage between believing spouses in 1 Corinthians 7:10. He goes on to say in the following verses that although he has no such command regarding believers married to unbelievers, he nevertheless can offer godly advice. Paul's transmission of Jesus' command, reflecting knowledge of historical Jesus traditions, helps explain why his moral teaching corresponds so closely with sayings of Jesus preserved in the narrative accounts.

Paul must have considered exhortations to holy living and brotherly love to be part of the gospel message. When the apostle Peter along with Paul's colleague Barnabas withdrew from table fellowship with Gentile believers in Antioch, Paul accused them of not "walking uprightly according to the truth of the gospel" (Gal 2:14; cf. Matt 8:11–12). The gospel was not just a set of propositions about Jesus but a summons to discipleship in all areas of life. Differences in emphasis would arise when teaching within a Jewish culture, as Jesus did, and addressing audiences in the Greco-Roman world, as did Paul.

Paul does not narrate post-resurrection appearances of Jesus, but he does summarize them in a way that aligns with the Four Gospels (1 Cor 15:5–7).

Under scrutiny, the gap between Paul's gospel message of salvation and that of the gospels has narrowed from a chasm to a crevice.[16] Paul's brief, emphatic statements about Jesus cannot be divorced from the context of the Scriptures of Israel or even from the rest of Paul's own teachings as contained in his letters.

Around the core of Paul's gospel, information about Jesus may be arranged in an expanded circle. From it we can sketch Jesus' earthly career in a way that corresponds closely to the fuller portrait in the life narratives.

In drawing these parallels over the course of the last two chapters, we have proven each point with references to those letters the academic community holds to be Paul's beyond dispute: Romans, 1 and 2 Corinthians, Galatians, Philippians, 1 Thessalonians, and Philemon. With more space than is available here, we could further expand the contacts between Paul's undisputed letters and the message of the Four Evangelists.

Purpose appears to be the last dividing line between Paul's gospel and the life stories. Paul preached so that his listeners would believe in Jesus and be saved, whereas the four Evangelists documented Jesus' earthly life. The purposes sound different, but if the Evangelists documented Jesus' life so that people would believe and be saved, then even less daylight is visible between their writings and what Paul preached.

We noted earlier that the writer of Luke's Gospel also wrote the book of Acts, in which Paul is shown preaching the gospel as he goes from city to city in Greece and Asia Minor. Of Paul's work in the city of Derbe, Acts 14:21 says, "When they had preached the gospel to that city and had made many disciples, they returned to Lystra and to Iconium and to Antioch."

The ninth chapter of Acts provides another description, saying, "And in the synagogues immediately [Paul] proclaimed Jesus, saying, 'He is the Son of God'" (Acts 9:20). The same chapter goes on to say that he "confounded the Jews who lived in Damascus by proving that Jesus was the Christ" (v. 22).

---

16 See, for example, Mitchell, "Mark, the Long-Form Pauline Εὐαγγέλιον."

Given Luke's definition of gospel preaching, consider how the life stories of Jesus unfold. As we read these narratives, we accompany their subject as he preaches and ministers. The stories build to certain climactic moments when the disciples or others recognize to some extent who Jesus is, or moments when Jesus actually discloses his identity.[17] One of these occurs after Jesus miraculously stills a raging storm on the Sea of Galilee, whereupon "those in the boat worshiped him, saying, 'Truly you are the Son of God' " (Matt 14:33).

John's Gospel describes the reaction of one of the disciples, Nathaniel, after Jesus demonstrates supernatural knowledge of where Nathaniel had been earlier in the day. "Nathanael answered him, 'Rabbi, you are the Son of God! You are the King of Israel!' " (John 1:49).

The Evangelists invite us to participate in moments of insight about Jesus' identity. They expect us to concur in the opinion of the disciples and others who declare Jesus to be the promised *Christos*, the coming king from the line of David, and the very Son of God. While many motives may have prompted the Evangelists, none was stronger than the desire to convince readers that Jesus is the Christ. The writer of John's Gospel is eager to tell us as much. "Now Jesus did many other signs in the presence of the disciples, which are not written in this book," he says, "but these are written that you may believe that Jesus is the Christ, the Son of God, and that believing you may have life in his name" (John 20:30–31).

If, as the book of Acts has it, Paul preached the gospel by persuading his listeners that Jesus was God's anointed, then the four Evangelists likewise preached—in writing.

A story in the Gospel of Mark further demonstrates the evangelistic purpose of the narratives. A woman comes to the house where Jesus is staying in Bethany outside Jerusalem and anoints him with costly oil. When some of those present object to this apparent waste of money, Jesus reproves them and commends the woman's actions, saying, "And truly, I say to you, wherever the gospel is preached in the whole world,

---

17 Examples of these disclosures are Matt 14:33; 16:16; 26:62; 27:54; Mark 8:29; 15:39; Luke 9:20; 22:70; John 1:34, 41, 49; 4:26; 6:69; 11:27.

what she has done will be told in memory of her" (Mark 14:3–9). If Mark believed that details of Jesus' ministry, such as the anointing at Bethany, were generally known to his readers, why would he bother to record them? By informing his audience about how and why the woman arrived to anoint Jesus, Mark is preaching the gospel, according to the logic of the passage itself.

Confirmation also comes from the first four verses of Luke's Gospel, where the author says he is writing an account of those events and beliefs that were "handed down," *paradidomi*, or delivered to Christians like himself by those who were "eyewitnesses and servants of the word [*logos*]" (Luke 1:1–4). In his well-known creedal formula, in 1 Corinthians 15:1-7, Paul likewise refers to the gospel, *euangelion*, as the "word," *logos*, he preached and that he had handed down, *paradidomi*, to the believers in Corinth.

In the first chapter of Romans, Paul tells Roman Christians who already call on Jesus as their Lord that he looks forward to "preaching the gospel," *euangelizo*, to them (Rom 1:15). To Paul, "the gospel" included spiritual instruction in various aspects of the faith.

We now can appreciate that the various embodiments of the Christian message, including the teachings of Paul, the teachings of Jesus, and the narrative accounts of Jesus, are the mingled currents of a single river rather than independent streams. The gospel message of salvation and the remembrances of Jesus' life represent points on a spectrum that has details at one end and short, summary statements at the other. The same unity holds across the spoken and written forms of the information.

In Chapter 1, we learned that the decree of Cyrus concerning the return of Jewish exiles was an expression of the pre-Christian gospel, good tidings for the people of God. The decree is cited in two passages in the Old Testament, both of which say that Cyrus had it "proclaimed" throughout his kingdom "and also put it in writing" (2 Chron 36:22–23; Ezra 1:1). From the beginning, therefore, the biblical gospel was both spoken and written.

Having established that the four Jesus narratives are forms of the gospel, what else should we know about them?

3

Dumas and the Synoptic Puzzle

Most people have heard of the adventure novel *The Three Muske-teers* by the French writer Alexandre Dumas. Set in the seventeenth century, the story is about three friends, Athos, Porthos, and Aramis, who are members of the French royal guard. The three are bound in a brotherhood represented by their famous motto, "One for all and all for one." In Dumas's book, we meet the trio by following the story of another young man, d'Artagnan, who comes to Paris seeking adventure in the king's service. The three guardsmen take d'Artagnan into their company, resulting in a group of four comrades—a trio plus one.

Dumas's fictional group bears a resemblance to the four New Testament gospels. The first three of these, Matthew, Mark, and Luke, are deeply interconnected. The Gospel of John belongs with them, yet it also stands at a distance from them. Scholars call the first three gospels "synoptic," meaning "together seen," because they are similar enough to be set alongside each other in parallel columns. In contrast, Matthew, Mark, and Luke do not include most of the ministry events and sayings recorded by John. The account of Jesus' arrest, trial, crucifixion, and resurrection is similar in all four gospels.

Because Matthew, Mark, and Luke sometimes use the same words, even identical or nearly identical phrases, many scholars believe that at least two of the authors consulted a common written source. Witnesses who independently describe an event will differ in their wording, and when they relate several anecdotes that lack an obvious chronology, they will not put them in the same order. When the testimony of two witnesses coincides closely in phrasing and order, it indicates a dependence of one upon the other or of both upon a third source of information.

In other parts of the Bible, the use of written sources does not undermine the claim of divine inspiration. The writer of 1 and 2 Chronicles sometimes copied information nearly word-for-word from the books of Samuel and of Kings. The same passage of prophecy occurs in Isaiah 2:2–4 and Micah 4:1–3, indicating that Micah adopted some language from Isaiah or vice versa. The New Testament books of 2 Peter and Jude are so similar, both in thought and in sequence, that one of the authors must have borrowed from the other.

According to the doctrine of inspiration, God could speak through the personalities of particular human writers, which is why there are differences in style and tone between different biblical books. Equally, God could guide a writer in reproducing the thoughts or copying the actual words of other writings. The Synoptic Gospels are a curious mixture of independent voices and shared material.

Careful comparison of similarities and differences among Matthew, Mark, and Luke points toward a certain order and relationship. Matthew's and Luke's versions of events tend to be smoother, less provocative, and more grammatical than those of Mark even though the wording is too similar to be coincidental. For example, when a storm arises on the Sea of Galilee and threatens to swamp the boat carrying Jesus and his disciples, Mark has the disciples expressing anger as well as fear; in Matthew and Luke, we only see the disciples' fear. It is easier to think that Matthew and Luke left out the anger they found in Mark's account than to think that Mark added it to what he found in Matthew or Luke.[18]

To cite another example, Mark 6:5–6 says that Jesus "could do no miracle" at Nazareth except some minor healings and that he was amazed at the unbelief of the people there. Matthew's parallel account says that Jesus "did not do many miracles" in that area "because of their unbelief" (Matt 13:58). Matthew makes it clearer than Mark that the people's lack of faith curtailed the extent of healings, not any limits to Jesus' abilities. Since we would expect the secondary writer to eliminate ambiguity rather than introduce it, the original version is probably Mark's.[19]

Besides a pattern of instances where Mark's record appears to be primary, it is unclear why Mark would deliberately omit the story of Jesus' miraculous conception if he were using either Matthew or Luke as a source. Finally, we saw earlier that Mark is the first of the Evangelists mentioned in our oldest historical source, Papias, even though Papias may imply that Matthew wrote first.

In addition to the material common to all three Synoptics, a few events and many sayings of Jesus that do not occur in Mark are shared between Matthew and Luke, and there is a certain order to them as well. This has prompted some scholars to propose a "sayings document," otherwise lost to history, called Q (Q standing for the German word *quelle*, source).

How might we explain the major items of external evidence and the internal characteristics of the gospels? Perhaps a well-trained Christian scribe decided to assemble a set of Jesus' sayings and some anecdotes. These notes were written in Greek, a language Jesus may have spoken occasionally even though he conversed mainly in Aramaic. The use of Greek is not surprising insofar as it is also the original language of three

---

18 Mark 4:38; cf. Matt 8:25; Luke 8:24. For other sarcastic remarks of the disciples in Mark that are absent from parallels, see Mark 5:31; 6:37; cf. Matt. 9:21; 14:17; Luke 8:45; 9:13 (in some late mss. the Markan comment has been assimilated to Luke 8:45).

19 A related item of evidence is the omission from Matthew and Luke of healings in Mark where Jesus uses ritual actions that might be misconstrued as magical (Mark 7:31–37; 8:22–26).

other distinctively Jewish-Christian documents: the Letter to the Hebrews, the Letter of James, and the Letter of Jude.

Possibly, a member of a scribal school associated with Matthew (Matt
23:34) who had the ministry notes saw the account written by Mark and
realized how strangely complementary the two writings were. The
notes had extensive teachings but not a complete narrative, while the
life story had a full and colorful narrative but only brief bits of teaching.
It would have been natural to combine the two along with other material into a longer account laden with Jesus' instructions. Because this
second narrative circulated widely among Jewish believers, it was
translated into Hebrew (or Aramaic in Hebrew script) at an early date,
giving rise to the belief that Matthew originally wrote in Hebrew.

Whatever the composition of Matthew looked like, a few years later
the author whom we now know as Luke likewise composed a life story
of Jesus. Luke drew from a version of the early ministry notes, from
Mark's Gospel, and from other material he had available. John's Gospel,
written later still, reflects memoirs dictated by the "beloved disciple," or
preserved from him, supplemented in a limited way by material from
Mark.

All theories about the creation of the gospels are speculative, and all
have weaknesses. The Synoptic materials are so densely interwoven
that the more someone studies them, the more complex the picture becomes.

Each of the Synoptic Gospels rearranges some events chronologically
versus the others. Each includes or leaves out details for reasons that
are not apparent. Each contains certain sayings, parables, and events
that occur only in that gospel. The birth narratives of Matthew and Luke
display large differences: the first has Magi traveling from the east, a
miraculous star, Herod's slaughter of innocent children in Bethlehem,
and the flight of Joseph, Mary, and Jesus to Egypt; Luke has none of
those events but rather the journey of Joseph and Mary from Nazareth
to Bethlehem in response to a census, the birth of Jesus in a stable, shep-
herds who see a heavenly chorus of angels, and the bringing of Jesus to

the temple after his circumcision—all of which are absent from Matthew.

When we bring in John's Gospel, the picture becomes even more complicated. In John, Jesus makes bold statements, such as "Before Abraham was, I am" and "I am the way and the truth and the life," that the Synoptics lack. Most of the miracles of John are also unique to that book. John alone reports that Jesus raised a man, Lazarus, from the dead after he had been in the tomb for more than three days. If Peter and Matthew had witnessed such a spectacular event, could they possibly forget it or feel that it was unworthy of mention when they themselves talked about what Jesus had done?

If the gospels are inspired, then at least some of the reasons for their differences lie within the unsearchable depths of God's wisdom. Recollections went from speaker's mouth to scribe's ear, from Hebraized Aramaic into Greek, from multiple sources into finished compositions, from independent documents into collections, and from collections into canon. Regardless of how convoluted the process was, it distilled the information into a form that unerringly serves God's purposes.

If the gospel accounts are not inspired, then their tangled connections, patchwork documentary histories, and the circumstances of their preservation and eventual recognition as Scripture owe ultimately to historical accident. Each of the writers intended for their work to be read and preserved. But no scholar or historian would be taken seriously if he or she argued that the writing, preservation, collection, and canonization of the New Testament gospels were engineered by humans as a single, coordinated project.

Is it plausible that a group of men acted in concert to create four life stories of Jesus that are related to each other yet differ in so many ways? Having done so would not have guaranteed that their accounts would become so popular, despite circulating independently, that all had to be equally honored by Christian leaders of later centuries. Nor could the authors or their patrons have foreseen, let alone dictated, the arrangement of their works in substantially their current form. What we know of history excludes such speculations.

The First Written Gospel

The obscure history of the canonical gospels eventually sparked debate over which of them was written first. For good reason, most scholars think that Mark was earliest, but they continue to discuss the subject.

Some years ago, I was turning that question over in my mind: "What was the first written gospel about Jesus?" We've seen that the missionary proclamation of Jesus as the Christ has always been to some extent biographical, and conversely that the New Testament life narratives had the purpose of declaring Jesus to be the Messiah, the Son of God. The description "gospel" is appropriate to both. Perhaps the first written gospel consists of those creedal statements from the pen of Paul that we reviewed in Chapter 1.

It then struck me that, if the four Jesus narratives are to be trusted, the first written gospel could not have been Mark or Matthew or John or even passages in Paul's letters. The first written gospel was a sign posted above Jesus' head when he was crucified. All four Evangelists refer to this sign, which probably was a rough wooden plaque. Here is what Mark says about it:

> And they crucified him, and divided his garments among them, casting lots for them, to decide what each should take. And it was the third hour, when they crucified him. And the inscription of the charge against him read, "The King of the Jews." (Mark 15:24–26)

Words for "write" or "inscribe" actually occur twice in verse 26. Literally it says, "And the inscription of the cause of him was inscribed, ' The King of the Jews.' "

Mark does not say where the charge was placed. Matthew says, "above his head"; Luke says, "over him"; John says, "on the cross." None have precisely the same wording of the plaque. Here is each rendering:

"This is Jesus, the King of the Jews" (Matthew 27:37)
"The King of the Jews" (Mark 15:26)
"This is the King of the Jews" (Luke 23:38)
"Jesus of Nazareth, the King of the Jews" (John 19:20)

Common to all is the title "The King of the Jews." Matthew adds the name Jesus, and John adds both Jesus and "of Nazareth" or "the Nazarene."

The king (not *a* king, but *the* king) over the Jews, that is, over the people of Judah, could be none other than the promised heir from the house of David, the Messiah. Does a declaration that Jesus is the king promised to Judah amount to a brief form of the gospel? If so, we might treat it as a curiosity. Ironically, the first person to exalt Jesus in writing was not a believer but one of his executioners.

Upon reflection, maybe we have stumbled upon more than a mere oddity. The four versions of the inscription collectively resemble the gospels that contain them, in that they differ but convey the same message. The gospels themselves differ in some respects while uniformly declaring Jesus to be the Messianic King and Savior. We begin to glimpse the unusual character of this sign. If the sign qualifies as a written gospel, then each version is a *mise en abyme*, that is, a projection of the whole into one of its parts; each is a miniature gospel-within-a-gospel, like the wheels within wheels described in the vision that opens the book of Ezekiel.

A notice or title on the cross is historically plausible. The second-century chronicler Cassius Dio, for example, tells of a runaway slave who was paraded through the Roman Forum bearing an inscription stating the reason he was to be crucified.[20] A few other ancient sources likewise confirm that a sign was occasionally created. However, these references are sufficiently rare that first-century writers would not have automatically included the item in a crucifixion scene. The sign, therefore, lends authenticity to the gospel accounts.[21]

Some commentators have explained the differences in the wording of the four versions of the sign as resulting from another detail from John's Gospel, the fact that the inscription was written in different languages. Their theory suggests that, even though all four gospels are in

20 Cassius Dio, *Roman History* 54.3.7.
21 Theissen and Merz, *The Historical Jesus: A Comprehensive Guide*, 458.

Greek, each individual author chose a different language version of the charge to render. That explanation is awkward and unlikely for a number of reasons, and unnecessary.

Start with the variation in Matthew and Luke consisting of the words "this is." These words could simply be a stylistic addition to form a clause. For example, when Jewish scribes in Egypt were translating the Hebrew Bible into Greek, they changed the phrase in Genesis 5:1, "The book of the generations of Adam," to a clause: "This is the book of the genealogy of man."

That leaves only the differences in Matthew's and John's versions compared to those of Mark and Luke. Besides the title King of the Jews, Matthew has the name Jesus, and John has "Jesus of Nazareth."

The difference between the versions with Jesus' name and those without it might result from abbreviation. Suppose the actual sign had the version with the most information, "Jesus of Nazareth the King of the Jews." Matthew and Luke both abbreviated and glossed to get their versions. Mark abbreviated it to the bare essence, "The King of the Jews." We find evidence bearing on this question in the Gospel of John. John alone relates the complaint of Jesus' opponents about the wording of the sign:

> Pilate also wrote a title and put it on the cross; it read, "Jesus of Nazareth, the King of the Jews" ...The chief priests of the Jews then said to Pilate, "Do not write, 'The King of the Jews,' but, 'This man said, "I am King of the Jews."'" Pilate answered, "What I have written I have written." (John 19:19, 21–22)

At face value the sign does not accuse Jesus of making himself king; it simply proclaims him as king. Jesus' enemies recognize the distinction and register a protest. As the priests object, they shorten the inscription to exactly the wording it has in the book of Mark. The gospel with the most elaborate rendering of the sign in effect endorses the simplest form as an abbreviation.

The four versions of the inscription exhibit both divergence and unity, but their differences are not essential. This makes the sign all the more intriguing as a convergence of history and literature. It gives us a greater incentive to confirm, if possible, that the sign qualifies as a written gospel.

A Rose or Messiah by Any Other Name

In the Shakespeare play *Romeo and Juliet*, Juliet famously says, "That which we call a rose by any other name would smell as sweet; So Romeo would, were he not Romeo call'd, retain that dear perfection which he owes without that title."[22]

To determine whether the sign on the cross is a gospel, we need to know to what extent certain titles of Jesus are interchangeable. As we discussed Chapter 2, Paul's gospel is often epitomized in titles given to Jesus: Jesus as Lord, Jesus the Son of God, and Jesus Christ. The most frequent of these is the last, that is, Jesus, who is the Christ, the Messiah. Here is one example from many:

> When I came to you, brethren, I did not come proclaiming to you the testimony of God in lofty words or wisdom. For I decided to know nothing among you except Jesus Christ and him crucified. (1 Corinthians 2:1–2)

Paul himself tells us that he preached Jesus as the Christ who was crucified to remove the world's sins. We saw previously that according to the book of Acts, Paul preached that Jesus was both the Christ and the Son of God (Acts 9:20–22). Another account of Paul's preaching in Acts identifies yet a third title:

> And Paul went in, as was his custom, and for three weeks he argued with them from the scriptures, explaining and proving that it was necessary for the Christ to suffer and to rise from the dead, and saying, "This Jesus, whom I proclaim to you, is the Christ." And some of them were persuaded, and joined Paul and Silas.... But the Jews were jealous, and taking some wicked fellows of the rabble...they dragged Jason and some of the brethren before the city authorities, crying, "These men who have turned the world upside down have come here also, and Jason has received them; and they are all acting against the decrees of Caesar, saying that there is another king, Jesus." (Acts 17:2–7)

---

22 *Romeo and Juliet*, Act 2, Scene 2.

Because Paul preached Jesus as the Christ, Jewish opponents charged that Paul was proclaiming Jesus to be king. The accusation made it sound as if Paul were promoting a human pretender to royal power, which he was not. But the charge had an element of truth because, as we learned earlier, the Messiah, or *Christos*, was expected to be a divinely powerful monarch.

Return for a moment to the first part of the Gospel of Mark. Mark sets the stage dramatically for Jesus' entrance by introducing John the Baptist, a prophet of repentance. We first see Jesus when he comes to John to be baptized. As he comes up from the water, Jesus has a vision of God's Spirit descending on him in the form of a dove, a vision that John the Baptist also sees, according to the Gospel of John (Mark 1:10; John 1:32). At the same time, a voice comes from heaven saying, "You are my beloved Son; with you I am well pleased." These words conflate two verses in the Old Testament, Psalm 2:7 and Isaiah 42:5, thereby uniting Psalms celebrating the triumph of the Messiah with the good news declarations of Isaiah.

Psalm 2 refers to the divine ruler as Messiah (or *Christos*), as King, and as Son of God (vv. 2, 6, 7). So closely does the Psalm associate these descriptions that they become synonymous. For God to say to Jesus, "You are my Son," is a way of designating him as Messiah and king. The Psalm says that he will reign from Zion, the highest point in Jerusalem, where Solomon's palace and the temple of Yahweh stood. This detail was important because not all of the kings of ancient Israel reigned from Zion.

Since its early history, Israel had consisted of two parts, corresponding to the two most prominent sons of Jacob, namely, Judah and Joseph (Josh 18:5). The descendants of Judah occupied the southern half of the land, while those of Joseph dominated in the north. King David only became ruler of the entire nation after he had first governed the territory of Judah for seven-and-a-half years (2 Sam 5:5). David's son Solomon ruled over the united kingdom, but during the reign of Solomon's son Rehoboam, the nation divided between north and south. Non-Davidic kings ruled the northern kingdom of Israel from its capital city of

Samaria until it was conquered by Assyria. The dynasty of David, from which the Messiah was promised to come, continued to rule over Judah until the deportation to Babylon.

As a consequence of the nation's history, there were kings of Israel's northern kingdom who had no part in the lineage of the coming Messiah. Once the Messiah arrived, he would reign over a united kingdom as had David and Solomon. But the Messiah would claim this legacy by virtue of being the rightful king of the people of Judah, a king of David's line, enthroned on the hill of Zion in Jerusalem. As we have seen, it was to the cities of Judah that Isaiah proclaimed the good news of God's visit (Isa 40:9).

To declare a man to be the rightful, that is, the Davidic, King of the Judahites, is the same as declaring him to be the Messiah, or Christ. Not only can we infer the equivalence from the scriptures we have just considered, but we can prove it by comparing specific passages in the gospels. To begin, here is Matthew's narrative of Pontius Pilate confronting the Passover crowd as they call for Jesus to be crucified, with emphasis added to the key words:

> Now the chief priests and the elders persuaded the people to ask for Barabbas and destroy Jesus. The governor again said to them, "Which of the two do you want me to release for you?" And they said, "Barabbas." Pilate said to them, **"Then what shall I do with Jesus who is called Christ?"** They all said, "Let him be crucified." (Matthew 27:20-22)

Now, look at the parallel passage in Mark:

> But the chief priests stirred up the crowd to have him release for them Barabbas instead. And Pilate again said to them, **"Then what shall I do with the man whom you call the King of the Jews?"** And they cried out again, "Crucify him." (Mark 15:11–13)

Where Matthew has, "Then what shall I do with Jesus who is called Christ?" Mark has, "Then what shall I do with the man whom you call the King of the Jews?" In the next chapter we'll consider why Matthew and Mark would choose to render this question differently, but between the first two Evangelists the terms "Christ" and "the King of the Jews" are treated interchangeably. It remains to be seen if the gospels offer further support for this point.

Multiple Proofs of the First Written Gospel

To the testimony of the first two gospels on the equivalence of "King of the Jews" and "Christ," we now add that of the Third Evangelist, Luke. What we are looking for occurs in the sequence from Luke 22:67–23:3. Here are four out of those eight verses:

> "If you are the Christ, tell us." But he said to them, "If I tell you, you will not believe." (Luke 22:67)

> And they all said, "Are you the Son of God, then?" And he said to them, "You say that I am." (Luke 22:70)

> And they began to accuse him, saying, "We found this man perverting our nation, and forbidding us to give tribute to Caesar, and saying that he himself is Christ a king." (Luke 23:2)

> And Pilate asked him, "Are you the King of the Jews?" And he answered him, "You have said so." (Luke 23:3)

In just eight verses, Luke takes us from the term "Christ" to "the Son of God" and finally to "the King of the Jews" as synonyms. In the following passage (emphasis added), Luke once again associates the titles:

> The soldiers also mocked him, coming up and offering him vinegar, **"If you are the King of the Jews, save yourself!"** There was also an inscription over him, "This is the King of the Jews." One of the criminals who were hanged railed at him, saying, **"Are you not the Christ? Save yourself and us!"** (Luke 23:36–39)

Bracketing the description of the sign are two derisive calls for Jesus to save himself, first because he is the reputed King of the Jews, second because he is the reputed Christ.

The Fourth Gospel has a dialogue set in the temple in which Jesus' adversaries demand that he tell them plainly whether he is the Christ. Jesus instead asserts his special relationship with his heavenly Father, prompting a charge of blasphemy. The sequence carries us from

"Christ" to "Son of God" in thirteen verses (John 10:24–36). Later, when Jesus is brought before Pilate, his enemies state their charge in two ways: that Jesus "made himself" (Greek, *heauton epoiesen*) God's Son and "makes himself" (*heauton poion*) king (John 19:7, 12).

The gospels so tightly connect the terms "Christ," "Son of God," and "King of the Jews" that any of them implies the others. By proclaiming Jesus as King of the Jews, the sign announces him as the Christ and so qualifies as a written gospel.

If any doubt remains, the Bible provides a final, independent confirmation that the sign is an expression of the gospel. In describing the sign, Matthew and Mark use a particular Greek word, *aitia.* Mark says, "And the inscription of the charge [*aitia*] against him read, ' The King of the Jews.' " The translation "charge" is misleading in that the definition of *aitia*, which is "cause" or "reason," is more general than a legal accusation.

A broad meaning of *aitia* is implied by an episode in Mark as compared to Luke. A woman suffering from a chronic hemorrhage is healed when she surreptitiously touches Jesus' cloak. When Jesus turns and confronts the woman, she reveals why she has touched him. What the woman discloses is the "whole truth," *pasan ten aletheian,* according to Mark, but it is the "reason," *aitia,* according to Luke (Mark 5:33; Luke 8:47). The word *aitia* is therefore capable of a double meaning in the case of the sign on the cross. What appears to be an accusation is instead the "whole truth" that, as Messianic King, Jesus must suffer for his people.

Aitia explicitly refers to the gospel message in two passages in the New Testament. The first is near the end of the book of Acts. The apostle Paul had been arrested in Jerusalem and falsely accused of desecrating the temple there. He appealed to Caesar Nero for justice and so was transported under guard to Rome. Upon arriving, Paul called the local Jewish elders and told them his story. Paul explains, "For this reason [*aitia*] therefore I have asked to see you and speak with you, since it is because of the hope of Israel that I am bound with this chain" (Acts 28:20). He arranged for them to return and hear his message at length.

Paul had suffered imprisonment over the "hope of Israel," the good news that in Jesus, God had kept his appointment with his people. At the very least, the gospel is included in the "reason" (*aitia*) of Acts 28:20. Paul may even be equating the "reason" with the "hope of Israel," the gospel for which he was persecuted and which he desired to share with the Jewish elders.

A passage in 2 Timothy contains a parallel thought to that of Acts 28:20 but is more definite in its language:

> ... But be a partaker of the afflictions of the gospel according to the power of God, who has saved us, and called us in Christ Jesus.... He has abolished death, and brought life and immortality to light through the gospel, of which I am appointed a preacher, and an apostle, and a teacher of the Gentiles; for which cause [*aitia*] I also suffer these things. (2 Timothy 1:8–12)

Undeniably, verse 12 says that the gospel of which Paul has been appointed a preacher is the cause, or reason, *aitia*, of his suffering. Unexpectedly, we have discovered a single word that describes both the content of the sign on the cross and the substance of the gospel, a word whose existence we would never have suspected by reading only English translations of the Bible. We have further confirmed our identification of the sign as a gospel.

A Christian gospel was written, then, even before Jesus died. But how complete could it be, consisting of just a few words designating Jesus as the Messianic King of the Jewish people? The sign communicates more than that because its context is not simply cultural. No one could have read it without taking in the whole scene, including the crucified figure over whom it hung. That brings it into close agreement with Paul's preaching. As Paul himself tells it, he confronted his audience with a crucified, dying Christ. "O foolish Galatians," he writes to believers in Asia Minor, "who has bewitched you, before whose eyes Jesus Christ was publicly portrayed as crucified?" (Gal 3:1).

In Jewish thought, a dying Messiah was an absurdity. The Messiah had to fulfill Israel's destiny and rule forever; therefore, he could not die. Peter, as quoted in the book of Acts, pointed out that this belief wasn't strictly true. What was impossible was for the Messiah to stay dead.

"This Jesus, delivered up according to the definite plan and fore-knowledge of God, you crucified and killed by the hands of lawless men," Peter tells the Pentecost crowd. "But God raised him up, having loosed the pangs of death, because it was not possible for him to be held by it" (Acts 2:23–24). The resurrection of the faithful at the end of time had been foretold in Isaiah and Daniel. The apostles claimed that Jesus was the first example, the pioneer of the resurrection to immortal life.

In Paul's message of "Christ crucified," the resurrection of Christ is always assumed or implied even if not stated outright, since the role of the Christ in God's purpose required his return from the grave. The sign on the cross therefore encapsulates Paul's gospel about God's crucified yet victorious Son.

4

Through the Eyes of D'Artagnan

We've come far on our journey toward that mysterious bit of information I mentioned in the introduction. We saw that the Christian gospel is a rebirth and expansion of God's promise that he would return the people of Judah to their land, meet them there, and use them to bless the peoples of the world.

We also learned that the message of Jesus himself, the message of Paul, and the written accounts of Jesus are all forms of the same Christ-centered proclamation. Finally, we established that within each of the written gospels is a miniature gospel, the sign on the cross. I've called the sign a *mise en abyme,* an abbreviated gospel-within-a-gospel that reflects both the unity and diversity of the documents that contain it. It seems odd to say that this first written gospel was the work of a pagan Roman, Pontius Pilate. It is surprisingly appropriate, however. The Gospel of John says that the Jewish high priest, Caiaphas, a man who conspired against Jesus and condemned him to death, was maneuvered by God into bearing witness to Jesus. Here is the passage:

> So the chief priests and the Pharisees gathered the council, and said, "What are we to do? For this man performs many signs. If

> we let him go on thus, everyone will believe in him, and the Romans will come and destroy both our holy place and our nation." But one of them, Caiaphas, who was high priest that year, said to them, "You know nothing at all; you do not understand that it is expedient for you that one man should die for the people, and that the whole nation should not perish." He did not say this of his own accord, but being high priest that year he prophesied that Jesus should die for the nation, and not for the nation only, but to gather into one the children of God who are scattered abroad. (John 11:47–52)

Caiaphas meant to say that, like any troublemaker, Jesus had to die for the sake of the nation's security, but his words actually bore witness to the sacrificial nature of Jesus' death. Pilate, another man who condemned Jesus, likewise unintentionally proclaimed that Jesus was the anointed king promised by God.

Pilate's testimony is also fitting in another respect. Matthew's Gospel says that within a year or so of Jesus' birth, astrologers from Arabia or Persia, the Magi, arrived in Judea inquiring about the birth of the king of the Jews. Gentiles were therefore the first to bear witness to that title, according to the gospels. Another Gentile, Pilate, applied the same words to Jesus at the end of his life. The testimony of the Magi only occurs near the beginning of the Four-Gospel Canon, while the fact that Pilate used the same words to describe Jesus is only noted at its end. Only the Fourth Gospel tells us exactly who wrote the sign or had it written. John says:

> Pilate also wrote a title and put it on the cross; it read, "Jesus of Nazareth, the King of the Jews." Many of the Jews read this title, for the place where Jesus was crucified was near the city; and it was written in Hebrew, in Latin, and in Greek. (John 19:19–20)

Besides the authorship of the sign, John includes another detail that we touched on briefly in the previous chapter when he says that the sign was written in a trio of languages. Another trio, the Three Musketeers, proved useful as an illustration of the canonical gospels because the three comrades-in-arms, Athos, Porthos, and Aramis, were later joined by d'Artagnan, so that the final group actually consisted of four musketeers. Recall also that readers of the novel meet the three musketeers through d'Artagnan's adventures, first seeing them through his eyes.

Readers who peer at the *titulus* through the lens of John's Gospel see that it, too, contains a threesome. The same title occurs in Hebrew, Latin, and Greek, offering us a new example of diversity in unity. Are the different languages just John's way of presenting Jesus as a universal Savior, as some scholars have argued? Or might they be connected to the trio of the Synoptic Gospels? We already know that the sign is a gospel and that its versions are in some respects reflective of the gospel narratives of Jesus.

It is time we look at what distinguishes one gospel narrative from another. Let's go back to a difference we discovered previously when we considered the question Pilate asked the Jewish crowd as he was deciding Jesus' fate. In Matthew he asks what he should do with the so-called Christ; in Mark he asks the people what he should do with the so-called king of the Jews. What would Pilate actually have said? "Christ" (Greek for "Messiah") has a Jewish background and probably had little meaning for a Gentile like Pilate; he would more easily have understood "king of the Jews." Mark's version is more realistic, but Matthew gives the exchange a more Jewish flavor by using the term "Christ."

It happens that this Jewish tilt is evident throughout the Gospel of Matthew. Both Matthew and Luke contain a genealogy of Jesus, but whereas Luke traces Jesus' lineage all the way back to Adam, Matthew focuses on two key figures, whom he identifies in the first line of his gospel: "The book of the genealogy of Jesus Christ, the son of David, the son of Abraham." The Jews proudly identified themselves as the children of Abraham, as we see from the following dialogue in John:

> Jesus then said to the Jews who had believed in him, "If you continue in my word, you are truly my disciples, and you will know the truth, and the truth will make you free." They answered him, "We are descendants of Abraham, and have never been in bondage to anyone. How is it that you say, 'You will be made free'?" (John 8:31–33)

The same Jewish pride in Abrahamic ancestry is reflected in Matt 3:9, Luke 3:8, and John 8:39.

Besides Abraham, Matthew mentions David, the founder of the dynasty of Judah. Along with his son Solomon, David is a standard-bearer of the Jewish people and a model of the coming Messiah. When we go through the gospels and simply count the number of times that the names Judah, David, and Solomon occur, we find that Matthew's total of twenty-six is nearly as great as the total of twenty-eight for the other gospels combined.

The religious identity of the Jews was also closely tied to the Torah, consisting of the five biblical books associated with Moses, along with the teachings of the Hebrew prophets. Matthew, in line with Jewish sympathies, speaks more highly of the Law of Moses than do Mark, Luke, and John. Matthew and Luke contain the saying that no particle of the law will fail, but only in Matthew does Jesus add that he has not come to destroy the law but to fulfill it, and that whoever teaches people to violate the law will be called least in the kingdom of heaven (Matt 5:17, 19).

Matthew makes more formal quotations from Israel's scriptures than do the other Evangelists, often in the course of explaining how Jesus fulfilled prophecy. We can measure the tendency by consulting a standard reference work for Old Testament quotations in the gospels.[23] By tallying these, we arrive at the following totals: Matthew, 66; Mark, 34; Luke, 43; John, 21.

Only in Matthew does Jesus issue a command that presupposes worship at the Jerusalem temple, when he says to reconcile with your brother before offering a gift at the altar. Again, only in Matthew does Jesus say that a rebellious member of the Christian congregation must be treated as if they were a Gentile (non-Jew) or a tax collector, reflecting peculiarly Jewish social attitudes (Matt 5:23–24; 18:17). The name "Matthew" itself is a Greek form of the Hebrew "Mattithiah" (1 Chron 9:31; Neh 8:4), whereas "Mark" and "Luke" are Greco-Roman names without Hebrew referents.

---

23 See Bratcher, *Old Testament Quotations in the New Testament*, 1–27.

Matthew's Gospel has so many unique marks of Jewishness that we cannot explore them all here. Even a cursory survey of Bible commentaries will confirm that Matthew's Jewish character is widely recognized.

One for All and All for One

It would be a mistake to conclude that the Jewish perspective of Matthew puts it at odds with Mark, Luke, and John. Like the other gospels, Matthew shows Jesus praising the faith of certain Gentiles. In Matthew Jesus predicts that Gentiles will have honored places in the kingdom of God, and at the book's end he commands his followers to preach to all nations (Matt 8:11; 28:19). Matthew's Jewish flavor is a matter of emphasis and style. The essential unity of all the gospels and the special relationship among Matthew, Mark, and Luke remain.

Something else about the Jewishness of Matthew's Gospel may now be apparent. It corresponds to the first of the three language versions of the sign as portrayed in John's Gospel, the version in Hebrew.

To link the Hebrew version of the title on the cross to Matthew is not to claim that Matthew's Gospel itself was written in Hebrew. The internal characteristics of the book point strongly toward Greek as the language of composition, even though the author shows a knowledge of Hebrew.[24]

A further complication is that John's Gospel in several places uses the word "Hebrew," *hebraisti*, to designate not Hebrew proper but the related language of Aramaic. Aramaic, in a Hebrew-influenced dialect, was widely spoken by the residents of Judea and Galilee in the first century. Some Bible translations even render the language list in John 19:20 as "Aramaic and Latin and Greek." The distinction, while worth noting,

---

24 Like the author of Hebrews, who also wrote in Greek, Matthew nevertheless understands and translates Hebrew names (Matt 1:21, 23; cf. Heb 7:2). Also, Matthew's Gospel was translated into Hebrew early and stands within the oldest stream of Jewish Christianity. See Craig Evans, "Jewish Versions of the Gospel of Matthew," *Mishkan* 38, 70–79.

is not critical to our discussion. Aramaic and Hebrew proper are both Semitic languages, unlike Latin and Greek.

The language in which Matthew was composed and the particular Semitic language John means by "Hebrew" are both less important than the undeniable Jewishness of Matthew compared with Mark and Luke. Only the first of the three language versions listed by John is appropriate as a cultural badge of the Jewish people. Matthew, being the gospel most closely aligned with Jewish culture, corresponds to the "Hebrew" (or Hebraized Aramaic) version of the title.

There are three gospels in the Synoptic Canon; there are three language versions in the miniature gospel on the cross. The First Gospel corresponds to the first language version.

What about the second of the Synoptic Gospels, Mark? Early Christian traditions are uniform in saying that Mark's Gospel was written in Rome. While Greek was spoken in Rome, as it was throughout the empire, the native language there and the language of the Roman officer corps, for example, was Latin. The plot of our study is now thickening. If Mark has closer connections to Roman culture than either Matthew or Luke, then the second gospel would correspond to the second language version of the inscription, the title in Latin.

The book of Acts mentions a disciple named John Mark (Acts 12:12, 25; etc.), whom Colossians 4:10 places with Paul during a time of Paul's imprisonment, presumably in Rome. Two other biblical texts link someone named Mark to Rome near the ends of Peter's and Paul's lifetimes (2 Tim 4:11; 1 Pet 5:13).[25]

The Bible therefore lends indirect support to traditions from the second century that give Mark's Gospel a Roman provenance. Most biblical scholars still favor Rome as the place where the Second Gospel was composed, but some argue that the author, whatever his true identity, lived and wrote in Syria or Galilee. Even if the dissenters are right,

---

25 "Babylon" in 1 Pet 5:13 is probably to be understood as Rome (cf. Rev 17:5, 9). Even if the authenticity of 2 Timothy and 1 Peter are questioned, these documents reflect early opinions about Paul's circumstances and associates during his imprisonment in Rome.

Mark's Gospel could still have a more Roman orientation than Matthew or Luke. What can we glean from the book itself on the subject?

Our first piece of evidence is Mark's relatively Gentile perspective. Roman culture was Gentile, not Jewish. Chapter 7 of Mark is especially telling on this point. In verses three and four, the author explains that Jews, particularly Pharisees, are careful to wash not just their hands but also food containers in order to maintain ceremonial purity. None of the other Evangelists feels such a need to educate readers about Jewish customs. Mark then shows Jesus upbraiding the Pharisees for their obsession with traditions. Jesus tells them that it is not what goes into a man that defiles him, but what comes out, meaning that it is not a person's diet but their words and actions that taint them with sin.

Besides Mark, only Matthew records the saying about what goes into a man and comes out of him, although Luke has a different saying that makes the same point. Between Mark's and Matthew's versions, each includes a statement that the other omits.

In Matthew 15:20, Jesus concludes the lesson by saying, "But to eat with unwashed hands does not defile a man." Matthew thereby limits the saying to the question of handwashing. The lesson in Mark lacks that concluding remark. Instead, Mark interjects an inference into Jesus' own explanation by adding, "Thus he declared all foods clean"—literally, "he cleansed all foods." Mark interprets Jesus as laying down a principle eventually reflected in the apostolic decision, years later, that Gentiles could become Christians without observing the kosher food laws (Acts 15:19–20).

According to the book of Acts, the conversion of the first Gentile to Christianity was preceded by a vision given to the apostle Peter (Acts 10:1–11:18). In the vision, a voice commands Peter to eat the meat of unkosher animals. When he recoils at this prospect, he is told to quit calling defiled what God has "cleansed," *katharizo*, the same word Mark uses to describe how Jesus "cleansed" all foods (Acts 10:15; Mark 7:19). After the vision, Peter visits the house of a Roman centurion, Cornelius, who believes the gospel and receives the Holy Spirit, as do his family and friends. The declaration in Mark's Gospel foreshadows the conversion of the Gentiles beginning with a Roman family.

Immediately after the lesson about foods and defilement, Mark's narrative follows Jesus on an excursion northward to the coastal towns of Tyre and Sidon deep in Gentile territory and then to the district of the Decapolis east of Galilee, another predominantly Gentile area. Luke omits this journey entirely. Matthew records the trip to Sidon but fails to mention the Decapolis. Near Sidon, Jesus heals the demonized daughter of a Gentile woman. Matthew simply calls this woman a Canaanite, since she is from the northern limit of the dwelling of the Canaanites (Gen 10:19); Mark identifies her as a member of the Greek-speaking Gentile community but takes pains to note that ethnically she is Syro-Phoenician (Matt 15:21–28; Mark 7:24–30).

In Matthew, Jesus three times refuses the Gentile woman's request for the healing of her daughter, first by remaining silent, then twice verbally. He tells her bluntly that he was sent only to Israel, meaning to Jews. In Mark, Jesus refuses the woman only once and does not say that he was sent to Israel only. In Matthew the woman addresses Jesus as "Lord, Son of David," a Jewish-oriented term; in Mark she implores him repeatedly but calls him simply "Lord." The two versions of the dialogue highlight the Gentile affinity of Mark in contrast to the Jewish perspective of Matthew.

Another example of Mark's Gentile sympathies is a dramatic scene in the Jerusalem temple. In all the Synoptics, Jesus drives merchants off temple grounds and quotes two scriptures against them, Isaiah 56:7 and Jeremiah 7:11. Here is what Jesus says according to each of the Synoptic Gospels:

> He said to them, "It is written, 'My house shall be called a house of prayer'; but you make it a den of robbers." (Matthew 21:13)

> And he taught, and said to them, "Is it not written, 'My house shall be called a house of prayer **for all the nations**'? But you have made it a den of robbers." (Mark 11:17; emphasis added.)

> . . . saying to them, "It is written, 'My house shall be a house of prayer'; but you have made it a den of robbers." (Luke 19:46)

Mark includes a phrase from the first text, Isaiah 56:7, that Matthew and Luke omit, the phrase "for all the nations."

Granting that Mark stands out among the Synoptics for its sympathetic stance toward non-Jews, what connections does it have specifically to the Roman people and culture?

Marcus Among the Eagles

The Gospels of Mark and Luke both bear Latin-based names, with Mark (or, Marcus) being the more famous of the two. One prominent example is Marcus Antonius, better known as Mark Antony, the lover of Cleopatra and rival to Octavius Caesar. Another is the Roman philosopher-emperor Marcus Aurelius. Between those historical Marks, chronologically, stands the Mark whose name is attached to the Second Gospel.

We will briefly consider four unique connections between Mark's Gospel and Roman culture. These are (1) Mark's introduction, (2) the mention of a name occurring elsewhere only in a list of Roman Christians, (3) the testimony of the centurion at the crucifixion of Jesus, and (4) Mark's more Latin-influenced vocabulary compared with that of the other gospels.

Let's review the beginning of Mark's Gospel by comparing it with that of Matthew:

> The book of the genealogy of Jesus Christ, the son of David, the son of Abraham. (Matthew 1:1)

> The beginning of the gospel of Jesus Christ, the Son of God. (Mark 1:1)

Matthew's opening words, "The book of the genealogy," *biblos geneseos*, are a Greek translation of Genesis 5:1. That verse, which we referenced briefly in Chapter 3, begins with the words, "The book of the generations of Adam." To adapt the Hebrew Bible this way right from the start is what we would expect of Matthew.

Mark's opening words, "the beginning of the gospel," do not occur in any Old Testament text. In the second verse, Mark quickly moves to a quote from Isaiah's gospel to Judah. However, the nearest parallel to the opening phrase is in a tribute to the Roman emperor Augustus known as the Priene Calendar Inscription, from Asia Minor. The inscription is an example of imperial propaganda that was carved into stone and set in public view in various parts of the empire.

The inscription from Priene celebrates Octavius Caesar, who became emperor after defeating Mark Antony and was given the title Augustus. It praises him as the savior who brought peace to the world, calling him divine and saying that his birth was "the beginning of good tidings." The relationship of the inscription to Mark's opening is the subject of an article by New Testament scholar Craig Evans.[26] Evans points out that Mark challenged Caesar's grandiose claims by asserting that Jesus was actually the divine savior whose coming was the beginning of good news.

We discover yet another link to Rome near the end of Mark's Gospel. Jesus must carry the horizontal beam of his cross from the governor's residence in Jerusalem to the execution site just outside the city. Having been beaten during a long, sleepless night and then brutally flogged, Jesus' physical stamina fails, and a bystander is pressed into service to help carry the crossbeam. Matthew and Luke identify this man only as Simon of Cyrene, a diaspora Jew from a Greek colony on the North African coast (Matt 27:32; Luke 23:26).

Mark alone adds that Simon was "the father of Alexander and Rufus," persons who apparently were known to at least some of his readers (Mark 15:21).[27] The name Rufus occurs in only one other place in the New Testament, near the end of Paul's letter to the Romans: "Greet Rufus, a choice man in the Lord, also his mother and mine" (Rom 16:13).

Rufus is a Latin cognomen, or nickname, meaning "red" or "redheaded." It belonged to several Roman statesmen and men of letters, including the great uncle of Julius Caesar, Publius Rutilius Rufus. Mark's Gospel therefore identifies a man with a quintessentially Latin, Roman

---

26 Craig Evans, "Mark's Incipit and the Priene Calendar Inscription," 67–81.
27 Alexander, the first son of Simon, likely remained in Jerusalem. An ossuary dating to the period is inscribed with the unusual name, "Alexander of Cyrene." See Kane, "The Ossuary Inscriptions of Jerusalem," 268–282.

name occurring nowhere else in biblical documents other than in a greeting to a Christian in Rome.

Our next connection between Mark and Roman culture is the confession of the centurion at the crucifixion. We noted in Chapter 2 that drama in the gospels peaks at moments when persons express faith in Jesus' identity as the Christ or the Son of God or the King of Israel.[28] In Matthew and John, the disciples make such declarations early in Jesus' ministry. In Luke, Peter acknowledges Jesus as the Christ, but no one confesses him using specifically the term "Son of God" until Paul does so in Luke's second volume, in Acts 9:20.

In Mark, Peter solemnly identifies Jesus as the Christ (Mark 8:29). No one else is shown making such a faith confession until Jesus is hanging on the cross. Black storm clouds have blocked out the sun, and Jesus cries out to God in his agony and dies. The Roman officer who is in charge of the crucifixion is moved to exclaim, "Truly this man was the Son of God!" (Mark 15:39). Mark structures his narrative so that the acknowledgment of Jesus' identity is shared between the Jewish apostle Peter and an unnamed Roman centurion.

Matthew's Gospel says that the centurion "and those who were with him" made this spontaneous confession, blurring the focus on the centurion himself (Matt 27:54). That exclamation is also less climactic because in Matthew, Peter and the disciples as a group had already confessed Jesus' divine sonship (Matt 14:33; 16:16). In Luke, the centurion's words are softened to "Certainly this man was innocent [or, righteous]," preserving the spirit of the statement but making it less directly Messianic (Luke 23:47). John does not record the statement at all. John's Gospel says that one of the soldiers jabbed Jesus' side with a spear, producing a flow of bloody serum ("blood and water," John 19:34–37), proving that Jesus had poured out his soul to death, as prophesied in Isaiah 53:12, and that he was pierced, as it says in Zechariah 12:10.

Mark not only reserves the confession of "Son of God" for the centurion, but in contrast to Luke and Matthew, he also makes the centurion

---

28 Expressions of faith must be distinguished from the defiant outbursts of possessed persons, which apparently were intended to prevent Jesus from revealing himself in his own time and way (Mark 1:24, 34; 5:7).

a crucial witness of the death of Jesus, as in John. Mark does not record the piercing of Jesus' side, but in Mark's telling, Pilate only releases the body of Jesus after calling the centurion and asking him to confirm that Jesus has died (Mark 15:44–45). This detail is not included in the other gospels.

Technically, the centurion does not confess that Jesus is "the Son of God," but "a son of God," or "God's Son," *uios theou.* This still designated Jesus as a divine figure. The same term occurs in John when Jewish leaders accuse Jesus before Pilate of making himself "God's Son," at which Pilate becomes fearful (John 19:7). The disciples, when struck with awe at Jesus' walking on the Sea of Galilee, use an equivalent expression (Matt 14:33).

Both Matthew and Luke relate the story of a centurion who asks Jesus to heal his servant from a distance because, as a Gentile, the centurion feels unworthy to invite Jesus into his house. Jesus says that not even in Israel has he found such faith. Mark lacks that episode, but he gives a Roman officer a special status by having him confess, despite his spiritual ignorance, the divine origin of Jesus.

Both Matthew and Luke refer to the centurion who asks Jesus for healing with the Greek word *hecatontarchays*, meaning commander of a hundred. Mark describes the officer at the cross with the word, *kenturion*, a Greek transliteration of the Latin *centurion*. That brings us to the fourth Roman connection, Mark's greater use of Latin-derived or Latin-influenced vocabulary as compared with the other Evangelists.

Where Mark says that Pilate wanted to satisfy the crowd by handing over Jesus, for example, and where he describes Roman soldiers doing Jesus mock homage, the phrasing looks suspiciously like Greek adaptations of Latin idioms (Mark 15:15, 19). Scholars will continue to debate the linguistic factors in particular cases to determine whether their accumulated weight supports the claim that Mark's Gospel was actually written in the city of Rome. It is enough for us to know its text bears more traces of Rome's language, Latin, than do the other three gospels, regardless of where Mark was written.

Rome's symbol of military power was the *Aquila*, the eagle figure atop the standards of Roman legions. When we survey the characteristics of the Synoptic Gospels, one of them stands closer to Roman culture than the others. The Second Gospel is the one that flies with the eagles.

Luke in the Heart of Achaia

We have now confirmed an unlikely correspondence between the first two gospels, Matthew and Mark, and the first two written entries of the miniature gospel, the sign on the cross. Matthew, the Jewish gospel, belongs naturally with the Hebrew writing on the sign; Mark, with the Latin. If the pattern holds, Luke's Gospel must correspond to the Greek writing.

We therefore should not be surprised to learn that Luke has the largest Greek vocabulary and the most sophisticated literary style of any of the Four Gospels. More than twice as many Greek words in the New Testament are exclusive to the Third Gospel as are to Matthew, Mark, or John.[29] Mark's writing style is simple, far from elegant, but he makes up for it by his ability to paint a vivid scene. Matthew's Greek is better and more grammatical than Mark's, but Luke surpasses them both.

Luke writes with at least two styles or voices. The first evokes the historical books of the Septuagint, the Greek Old Testament. The second is closer to the style of the classical Greek writers, especially the historians.

Alone among the gospels, Luke begins with a formal introduction. The author dedicates his work to someone named Theophilus, who seems to be a high-ranking public official. The name Theophilus means "lover of God," which makes Luke's words appropriate for every godly-minded reader. In the first four verses of his gospel, Luke tells Theophilus that while others have compiled narratives of these events

---

29 Distinctive vocabulary in numbers of words exclusive to each gospel: Matthew, 112; Mark, 79; Luke, 261; John, 112. See Grant, *A Historical Introduction to the New Testament*, 95, 102, 109, 121. Available online at NTSLibrary.com.

based on information from eyewitnesses and ministers of the word, it seemed good to him also to write an orderly account, having done careful research, so that Theophilus will know the truth of what he has been told.

A statement of purpose similar to that of Luke can be found in the first section of *The History of the Peloponnesian War* by the Greek general-turned-historian Thucydides, writing in 431 BCE. Thucydides says that he has reconstructed the history of the war between Athens and Sparta from his own memories and eyewitness testimony, being careful to compare accounts to ascertain the facts. He says that he will be content if his work is deemed useful by those who wish to know the truth about the past and thereby gain insight into the future.[30] It's easy to see how Luke follows in the same tradition in the opening to his gospel.

Luke's quasi-historical approach is evident in the account of the early church in Acts as a follow-up to the story of Jesus. Luke anchors both stories in the wider world with information about Gentile rulers, dates, and places.[31] In this, again, Luke emulates the Greek chroniclers such as Herodotus and Thucydides, who set the tone for modern historical writing with their ideal of objectivity.

Luke's perspective is more Jewish than Mark's but more Gentile-sympathetic than Matthew's. Luke preserves material that is noticeably favorable toward Samaritans, the descendants of the people of the northern kingdom of Israel who lived in the district between Judea and Galilee. The well-known parable of the Good Samaritan, for example, only occurs in Luke. Oddly, this Samaritan sensitivity also has a Greek aspect in that Greek cultural influence seems to have been stronger on the Samaritans than on the Jews.[32]

Luke's Gospel has yet other connections to Greek culture. In Matthew and Luke, Jesus explains his desire to reach out to rejected members of

---

30 Thucydides, *The History of the Peloponnesian War,* 1.20–23.

31 Luke includes historical references more consistently than any other New Testament writer. E.g., Luke 1:5; 2:1–2; 3:1–2; Acts 4:5–6; 5:36–37; 12:20–23; 18:2; 23:23–26:32.

32 Tellingly, Samaria was evangelized by the disciple Philip, a deacon of the Greek-speaking part of the Jerusalem church (Acts 6:1–5; 8:5–12).

Jewish society by telling the parable of the shepherd who has one hundred sheep (Matt 18:12–13; Luke 15:4–6). When one sheep strays, the shepherd leaves the ninety-nine, searches out the lost sheep, and rejoices. In Matthew, the shepherd simply finds the sheep. In Luke, the shepherd puts the sheep on his shoulders and carries it home. This added detail does not come from the Old Testament. Isaiah 40:11 says that the divine shepherd carries the lambs in his bosom, cradling the animals in front of his body.

The Greeks had a portrayal of Hermes, the divine messenger, called the *kriophoros*, the "ram-bearer." It is preserved in statues and carvings of a shepherd carrying a ram or lamb, most often over his shoulders. This figure had associations with sacrifice, but just as prominently it was a symbol of compassion.[33] While Mark's Gospel shows that Christ, not Caesar, is the world's savior, Luke shows that the symbol of loving-kindness known for centuries in Greece had its true counterpart in Jesus, the Good Shepherd.

Paul provides another point of contact between Luke and the Greeks. In 1 Corinthians Paul contrasts the spiritual priorities of Jews and Greeks by saying, "For Jews demand signs and Greeks seek wisdom, but we preach Christ crucified, a stumbling block to Jews and folly to Gentiles but to those who are called, both Jews and Greeks, Christ the power of God and the wisdom of God" (1 Cor 1:22–24).

Paul sometimes uses "Greek" simply to mean Gentile. In the verse quoted above, he shows that the ethnic Greeks had set the spiritual agenda for the non-Jewish world as surely as their language dominated the field of literature. Even today, mentioning the subject of philosophy is likely to call to mind the early Greek thinkers Socrates, Plato, and Aristotle. The word "philosophy" is itself Greek, a compound of the words *philos*, affection, and *sophia*, wisdom. A philosopher is a lover and seeker of wisdom.

The book of Acts, chapter 17, depicts Paul as visiting the ancient seat of philosophy, the city of Athens in Achaia, the Greek heartland. Athens was named for Athena, the Greek goddess of wisdom. Standing on Mars

---

33 See Wilken, *The Christians as the Romans Saw Them*, 81.

Hill, the Areopagus, Paul comments on the religiousness of the Athenians as evidenced by the abundance of idols in their city. Paul has even chanced upon an altar to an unknown god, and this overlooked deity, he says, is the one whom he is preaching. He then briefly presents the gospel about Jesus.

As he paints the scene in Athens, the Third Evangelist includes Epicurean and Stoic philosophers in Paul's audience. The members of these philosophical schools were known to be skeptical of popular Greek notions about the gods. What would Paul's words mean to those Greek intellectuals who sought after wisdom? Although the philosophers speculated about the existence of God or the gods, their objects of devotion were really wisdom and knowledge. Insofar as the philosophers, despite all their learning, remained ignorant of divine wisdom, they too worshiped at the altar of an unknown god. What has this to do with Luke's Gospel?

New Testament scholar Ben Witherington, in his book *Jesus the Sage: The Pilgrimage of Wisdom*, shows that the wisdom theme is woven into the Four Gospels.[34] Matthew seems more devoted to proverbial Hebrew wisdom, which is less analytical than its Greek counterpart. However, when we simply search the gospels for the biblical terms for "wisdom" and "wise man," they occur more often in Luke than in Matthew, Mark, or John. Luke tells us twice that as Jesus grew to manhood, he increased in wisdom (Luke 2:40, 52).

After warning his disciples that they will be dragged into court, Jesus reassures them that they need not worry about how to answer the charges against them. In Matthew's and Mark's record of this instruction and in Luke's first version of it, Jesus tells the disciples that God's Spirit will give them what they are to say in court.[35] Luke alone has a second version of the saying, in which Jesus says that when the disciples appear before kings and governors, "I will give you a mouth and wisdom [*sophia*], which none of your adversaries will be able to withstand or contradict" (Luke 21:12–15). This statement does not exclude the Holy

34 Witherington, *Jesus the Sage: The Pilgrimage of Wisdom* (Augsburg Fortress, 1994).
35 Matt 10:17–20; Mark 13:11; Luke 12:11–12.

Spirit, but it identifies Jesus himself as the giver of superior wisdom during times of trial.

The companion volume to Luke's Gospel, the book of Acts, describes the martyr Stephen as being filled with wisdom (Acts 6:3, 8, 10). When opponents charge Stephen with blasphemy and drag him before the Jewish high council, he reviews Israel's history leading up to the killing of the righteous one, Jesus, after which Stephen himself endures a martyr's death (Acts 6:9–7:60). Wisdom, named as such, is more prominent in Luke's writing than in that of the other Evangelists.

With a tentative identification of Luke as the most Greek-oriented of the Synoptic Gospels, an alignment begins to emerge between that trio of documents and the inscription on the cross as described in the Fourth Gospel.

5

The Hologram Crystallizes

In Chapter 4, we began to examine evidence of Luke's affinity for Greek language and culture. Seemingly minor details confirm our initial impression. Whereas according to Matthew, the wise man builds his house on the rock, Luke says the man must dig deep to build on bedrock (Matt 7:24; Luke 6:48). In the rugged landscape of Judea, rock is nearer the surface than it is in Greece, where the covering of topsoil is thicker.[36]

We have already seen that the attention Luke pays to wisdom, compared to the other three gospels, aligns with the Greek interest in philosophy, the search for wisdom. The prime example of the wisdom theme in Luke is a passage in which Jesus indicts the Jewish religious leaders for their arrogance and hard-heartedness and predicts that they will persecute his representatives just as their ancestors attacked the prophets. He says, "Therefore also the Wisdom of God said, 'I will send them prophets and apostles, some of whom they will kill and persecute'" (Luke 11:49).

---

36 In another example, Mark refers to "digging" through the mud-and-thatch roof of a peasant house in Galilee (Mark 2:4). Luke describes removal of the tiles that relatively wealthy Greek readers would picture as constituents of the roof (Luke 5:19). The New Testament singles out Greeks as comparatively affluent (1 Cor 4:8; Rom 15:26–27).

Our initial impression when reading the wisdom passage in Luke 11 is that Jesus is quoting Scripture, but there is no such text in the Old Testament, nor is Scripture elsewhere introduced as something said by the "Wisdom of God." The context of the statement refers to what Jesus himself had done. In the two previous chapters of Luke, Jesus had sent out representatives on preaching tours. He had first commissioned his core group of twelve followers, and sometime afterward, seventy other disciples. Jesus commanded both groups to preach the gospel, cautioning them that they would not always enjoy a favorable reception (Luke 9:3–5; 10:2–11). All these missionaries, by carrying a divine message, functioned as prophets, with the core group of twelve also being apostles.

In Luke 11:49, Jesus seems to say that God's wisdom is on display in his own decision to send out missionaries knowing that they would be persecuted. Dramatic confirmation comes from Matthew's version of the same saying. In Matthew, Jesus says, "Therefore I send you prophets and wise men and scribes, some of whom you will kill and crucify, and some you will scourge in your synagogues and persecute from town to town" (Matt 23:34). Matthew shows directly that Jesus is the sender of missionaries; in Luke, Jesus sends them not just according to God's will but as the very personification of divine wisdom. Luke's Gospel therefore reflects Paul's declaration that Jesus is "the power of God and the wisdom of God" (1 Cor 1:24).

As we learned in the previous chapter, Paul said that the Jews demand signs and the Greeks look for wisdom. Matthew, the most Jewish of the gospels, shows the Jews demanding a sign from Jesus twice (Matt 12:38; 16:1). In Mark and Luke, they ask for a sign just once (Mark 8:11; Luke 11:16). However, we've observed that Luke, the most Greek of the gospels, prominently features wisdom. In Luke, Jesus grows in wisdom, promises to be the source of supernatural wisdom for his disciples, and even speaks as Wisdom personified. Just as Jesus was the sign of God's power and salvation that the Jews stumbled over blindly, he was also the wisdom that the Greeks otherwise sought in vain.

The object of our investigation now stands revealed. The sign on the cross is a miniature written gospel within each larger gospel, and the one non-Synoptic gospel, John, contains a tripartite sign in which each language version of the messianic declaration corresponds to one of the three Synoptics: the Hebrew to Matthew, the Latin to Mark, and the Greek to Luke. The multi-faceted or multi-dimensional representation within John is what makes the sign on the cross, as a feature common to the four narratives, a literary "hologram." The Fourth Gospel, by adding to the title the information that Jesus was "a Nazarene" or "of Nazareth," distinguishes itself in the course of representing the Synoptic trio, making its version of the sign a *mise en abyme,* an internal self-reflection, of the complete Four-Gospel Canon.

Early traditions about where the gospels were written largely fall into line with the hologram. The prime example is in a series of notes to the gospels, found in some ancient Latin Bibles, called the Anti-Marcionite prologues. The prologue to Luke says that while Matthew wrote his gospel in Judea and Mark wrote his in Italy, Luke was moved by the Holy Spirit to write his in Achaia.[37] In biblical terms, Achaia took in all of central and southern Greece, including the great Greek cities of Athens and Corinth. The Lucan prologue conforms to the Synoptic pattern so closely as to leave us wondering how the hologram went unnoticed for such a long time.

Thus far we have not indulged in what skeptics call "prophecy mining" by arbitrarily connecting the Synoptic Gospels with an unrelated passage of the Bible. The facts, once discovered, come together organically. Any amount of circumstantial evidence might be coincidental, but if so in this case the coincidence extends to the cultural affinities of the Synoptic Gospels and early traditions concerning them, the language variants listed in John, and the appropriateness of the designation "gospel" for both a spiritual biography of Jesus and the inscription on the cross. The entire body of evidence is larger yet, as we will see.

The alignment of the Synoptics' characteristics would be impressive even if the sequence of the languages and of Synoptics did not match,

---

37 See Heard, "The Old Gospel Prologues," 7–9.

but it does match: Hebrew-Latin-Greek; Matthew-Mark-Luke. There is only one chance in six that these two sets would line up by chance, aside from each by chance having three members.

However, readers checking my scriptural references in the King James Bible might be confused because, unlike modern language versions, it does not read "Hebrew, Latin, and Greek" in John 19:20 but "Hebrew and Greek and Latin." The same readers might also have discovered that in the King James Bible, John is not the only gospel to list the different languages on the sign. Luke 23:38 in the KJV adds the language information as follows: "And a superscription also was written over him in letters of Greek and Latin and Hebrew, 'This is the king of the Jews.' "

The different readings in the verses cited above reflect the wording of many medieval New Testament manuscripts, in particular those used by the Catholic scholar Erasmus to prepare the first reconstructed Greek text of the New Testament in the year 1516. In addition to the differences in wording in John 19:20 and Luke 23:38, there are important manuscripts of what is called the Western Text type that arrange the gospels not in the order Matthew-Mark-Luke-John but instead Matthew-John-Luke-Mark. How do these variations affect the gospel hologram?

Through a Glass, Darkly

The holographic pattern is less obvious in Bibles with the variants we have identified than it is in modern translations, where it stands out boldly. The darkening of the hologram in the later manuscript tradition is perhaps the main reason why, for hundreds of years, commentators failed to grasp the connection between the narrative gospels and the writing posted on the cross.

The mechanics and psychology of manuscript transmission explain why the hologram was obscured. In the early days of Christianity, copying would have been done by Christian scribes with varying levels of skill or else by hired commercial scribes who did not appreciate the sacred nature of the documents they handled.

Despite the value placed on accuracy in copying, errors, mostly of spelling and word order, multiplied quickly. Chapter and verse divisions as we know them today did not exist to facilitate the checking of manuscripts against one another. Literary precedents could act as rough guides, but there were no precise rules for arranging the gospels and apostolic letters once they began to be collected into codices, that is, leafed pamphlets and books rather than scrolls. The earliest known fully bound Bibles of the kind we take for granted were created in the late third or early fourth centuries and must have been exorbitantly expensive, treasured, and uncommon possessions at that time.

While the biblical text remained substantially intact up to the time of the Middle Ages, the accumulation of thousands of small changes resulted in divergent manuscript traditions. By patiently comparing the surviving documents word-by-word, even letter-by-letter, scholars of later times have sought to determine where errors have crept in and what are likely to be the original readings.

The more manuscripts that are available for study and the older they are, the more accurate the reconstructions that textual scholars can provide to translators. Erasmus consulted a half-dozen or so relatively late manuscripts to create what came to be known as the Received Text, upon which Bibles such as the King James Version are based.

The nineteenth-century German scholar Constantin von Tischendorf played a crucial role in shedding light on the New Testament. Tischendorf tirelessly sought and compared manuscripts with the goal of establishing a more accurate biblical text. He is best known for a discovery he made while visiting the world's oldest monastery, St. Catherine's, on Mt. Sinai in Egypt.

After seeing priceless pages of a Greek Old Testament in a wastebasket, Tischendorf questioned the monks about ancient manuscripts they might possess. Eventually he was shown a nearly complete and extremely old vellum Bible in Greek. Clues from the material and lettering dated this Bible to the fourth century, making it hundreds of years older than the manuscripts consulted by Erasmus.

The Vatican library in Rome held the only other manuscript as old as the one Tischendorf discovered at St. Catherine's. Vatican authorities had tightly restricted the access of biblical scholars to this invaluable resource. Just a year before Tischendorf visited St. Catherine's, the Vatican librarian allowed him to view this other manuscript only long enough to copy a few verses.

Perhaps partly in response to Tischendorf's discovery at Sinai, Vatican authorities finally published a critical edition of their manuscript over the next three decades. These two vellum Bibles, known respectively as Codex Sinaiticus and Codex Vaticanus, both date to just three hundred years after the deaths of the apostles Paul and Peter. They are considered by the majority of textual scholars to be among the most important documents we possess for producing an accurate text of the New Testament. Furthermore, from the late 1800s onward, fragments of the Bible written on papyrus were uncovered in Egypt, and these, along with later manuscripts, are widely used by modern textual scholars.

Many New Testament verses in Codex Sinaiticus and Codex Vaticanus read slightly differently from the way they do in most later copies. One of these verses is John 19:20, describing the languages of the sign on the cross. Instead of reading "Hebrew, Greek, Latin," Sinaiticus and Vaticanus read "Hebrew, Latin, Greek." The papyrus manuscript designated P66, which is likely even older than Sinaiticus and Vaticanus, also supports that order. This united testimony from an early date explains why modern Bibles list the languages in a different order than the King James Bible.

Assuming the original order was Hebrew-Latin-Greek, why would someone change it? Such a change would be small and seemingly harmless. Since no information was lost or added, a scribe could justify the rearrangement if he felt it was warranted.

By and large, the Bible was originally written in just two languages. What we call the Old Testament was written in Hebrew (with a few short passages in Aramaic), and the New Testament that followed it was written in Greek. Notice that order: Hebrew, Greek. It also conforms to the preaching of the gospel first to the Jews, the people of the Hebrew language, and then to the Gentiles, the Greek speakers of the first century. Paul himself had written that salvation was offered to those with faith, the Jew first and also the Greek (Rom 1:16). The order Hebrew-Greek-Latin, putting the biblical languages first, probably felt more natural to the scribe who altered the text. The revision also brought the list into line with the historical appearance of the Bible first in the Hebrew language, then in Greek, and finally in Latin translation.

The greater likelihood that a scribe would alter "Hebrew, Latin, Greek" to "Hebrew, Greek, Latin" rather than doing the reverse helps confirm that the older reading is original. A seemingly inconsequential change in the order of two small words had the effect of clouding the gospel hologram for centuries.

The Errant Copyists

What about the other difference we noted between modern Bibles and older Bibles, the listing of the three languages in Luke 23:38? That change smears out the tripartite character of the sign between the Gospels of Luke and John. The evidence from our earliest manuscripts points to the language listing in Luke as a later addition to the original text.

As a scribe copied a particular gospel, he would note that it did not contain certain passages from one or more of the other gospels. Occasionally it lacked a passage that he felt was important to the story of Jesus or a detail that he found especially noteworthy. The temptation then arose to add this information to the gospel he was copying. After all, he wouldn't be adding his own words; he would be including words he already knew to be part of inspired Scripture. In the scribe's mind, he might be restoring what ought to be there. The result was a process of assimilation, the transfer of passages and wording between gospels.

An example of an assimilated passage is a detail of the crucifixion that, like the three languages on the sign, is unique to John. As we saw in Chapter 4, John 19:34 says that one of the soldiers guarding Jesus pierced his side with a spear, causing bloody serum to flow out. At least one early scribe found this detail so compelling that he inserted it into

Matthew at 27:49. This insertion even occurs in Codex Sinaiticus and Codex Vaticanus, both of which lack the insertion at Luke 23:38.

It is understandable, if unfortunate, that scribal copyists were tempted to import the image of blood flowing from Jesus' side into Matthew. The multilingual sign on the cross, although a less dramatic detail, was likely to stick in the minds of scribes, who worked with language for a living. Apparently, one who knew from reading John that the inscription was written in three languages felt no qualms about adding that information to Luke.

The image of someone writing the sign on the cross must have been firmly in the scribe's mind while he was making the addition. These early copyists tediously created one letter at a time, so the scribe was lettering in Greek as he inserted the words that the sign was "lettered in Greek and Latin and Hebrew."

Our last variation related to the hologram is not a difference in the order of words but of entire books, inasmuch as some manuscripts have the gospels in an unfamiliar order: Matthew, John, Luke, and Mark. These manuscripts of the Western Text Type are in a minority, however. Most Greek manuscripts containing the Four Gospels have them in the familiar order, and that holds for ancient ones, including Sinaiticus and Vaticanus. We can trace this order back earlier still, to the last quarter of the second century.[38]

In Chapter 3, we saw that the order in which the gospels were written, or at least the order in which they assumed their completed forms, was probably Mark, Matthew, Luke, and John. The ages of the documents, though important, were not the only factor in determining their order in early collections. The honor accorded the original apostles of Jesus made it appropriate to give first place to a book bearing an apostolic name. Furthermore, there is the principle we've discussed that God revealed himself first to the Jews and afterward to Gentile peoples.

Not only did the Gospel of Matthew bear the name of an apostle, it was also the most Jewish in its perspective. It made a fitting bridge be-

---

38 The work *Against Heresies* (3.1.1) by Irenaeus of Lyon, from around 180 CE, lists the order of writing as Matt-Mark-Luke-John, probably reflecting the order of their occurrence in a bound edition.

tween the Scriptures of Israel and the Christian sacred writings. And, to be fair, Matthew could well be the direct literary descendant of the earliest notes about Jesus. These were valid reasons for switching Matthew with Mark, but in other respects the order we see in bound manuscripts likely owes to the order of composition.

When monks of the western manuscript tradition revised the order of the canonical gospels, they gave the two apostles precedence, so John was moved up next to Matthew. Luke's Gospel was longer and more elegantly written than Mark's, besides being more popular, so Mark's Gospel was demoted to last place. Although this order makes some sense, it could not supplant the older arrangement.

The Deepening Mystery

We have traced the gospel hologram from its roots in ancient Israel through the storms and afflictions of the Jewish people, down the dusty roads of Galilee and the crowded streets of Jerusalem. We followed it as it fanned out through the Roman Empire with the first Christian missionaries, went from mouth to papyrus to vellum, and survived in the libraries and storerooms of all-but-forgotten monasteries.

What we have not yet encountered is a natural explanation for the presence of a holographic record, at low resolution, of the first three gospels within the Fourth Gospel of the New Testament. Far from being a transparent fiction, the sign on the cross as described in John is plausible as history. Simultaneously, evidence demonstrates it to be an ideal medium for representing a larger reality.

Further below we will take up coincidence as a way to account for so many clues pointing in the same direction, but what non-coincidental explanations are possible? One would be collusion. Did the four Evangelists somehow communicate with each other before they wrote their accounts and agree to coordinate their efforts in this clever, subtle way? As discussed in Chapter 3, that idea is unlikely in the extreme.

In 2009, textual scholar Bart Ehrman published a book titled *Jesus, Interrupted*. Among the points Ehrman makes in the book, as in his university course on the New Testament, is that ordinary Christians remain largely ignorant of the conclusions of academic scholarship regarding the documentary histories of the gospels and other New Testament books.[39]

To Ehrman, the gospels contain contradictions that are impossible to reconcile. Further, Ehrman believes that any effort to harmonize the gospels is misguided. He emphasizes how far removed the Evangelists were from the historical person of Jesus and that each interpreted the story of Jesus uniquely. In spite of sharing many stories and sayings, the gospels represent fundamentally different perspectives, argues Ehrman, who regards them as islands unbridgeably separated from each other.

Ehrman, not being a Christian, reads the Bible skeptically. Apparent contradictions between the gospels, though challenging, do not alter the thrust of the narratives, especially when we consider the flexible literary approach the Evangelists took to their subject. The gospels complement and enrich rather than diminish each other. Ehrman is right in one respect. At a minimum, the past two centuries of historical criticism have conclusively demonstrated that the gospels are too divergent to have been planned as parts of a collected work.

In *Jesus, Interrupted*, Ehrman admirably sums up the long and humanly unpredictable process that resulted in the New Testament canon.[40] In the late first and early second centuries, Christians scattered across the expanse of the Roman Empire lacked a governing institution with the organizational unity and technical means to screen, select, and officially promote certain documents rather than others. During those early decades, the opinions of local Christian scribes, teachers, and bishops shuffled certain books to the top of the stack.

By the mid-second century four of the Jesus stories had won respect on all sides, but as late as the end of that century the extra-canonical Gospel of Peter had some advocates associated with otherwise orthodox churches.[41] Books such as the Gospels of Thomas and of the Hebrews

---

39 Bart Ehrman, *Jesus, Interrupted* (HarperCollins, 2009) 21.
40 Timothy Beal, another academic, targets the Bible's messy documentary history in the title of his own book, *The Rise and Fall of the Bible: The Unexpected History of an Accidental Book* (Houghton Mifflin Harcourt, 2011).

would continue to circulate on Christianity's wide fringes for another century and a half.

If the four Evangelists and their patrons could not have deliberately built the hologram into their works from the start, could someone at a later time have inserted the title on the cross into Matthew, Mark, Luke, and John? Imagine trying to accomplish that after the Four Gospels were commonly accepted. Copies then would already exist in far-flung locations, from Rome to Antioch to Alexandria. No one could expect that changes made in one or two manuscripts would supplant the original readings.

The various passages about the sign on the cross are stable throughout the manuscript tradition. The only major variants are those we have already discussed: the different order of languages in later copies of John and the insertion of the language list into Luke. Minor variants that insert "this is" into Mark 15:26 to read "This is the King of the Jews" and "Jesus" into Luke 23:38 to read "This is Jesus, the King of the Jews" are assimilations in which wording was transferred between gospels.

A few manuscripts have "superscription" instead of "inscription" or an even less important prepositional difference. No textual scholar would entertain the speculation that verses about the title on the cross were seamlessly added to all four gospels while they were circulating. The dozens of additional verses that establish Matthew's cultural orientation toward Hebrew, Mark's toward Latin, and Luke's toward Greek make that explanation even less plausible.

Gospel Verses and Lottery Tickets

Let's persist a bit further in trying to explain the gospel hologram as a natural occurrence. Once the gospels were circulating, no one could have tampered with them, but couldn't someone have done so earlier? That would mean predicting which stories of Jesus would eventually be regarded as inspired. It would also require knowing where the gospels were written, gaining access to each one at an early stage, and interfer-

---

41 Besides the Gospel of Peter, other non-canonical gospels were known to bishops of the fourth century. See Eusebius, *Ecclesiastical History* 3.25; 6.12.

ing with the copying process. Again, no competent scholar or historian, or anyone informed about the culture in which the gospels were created, would deem that scenario realistic.

Conspiracy, then, is not a live possibility, whether at the time the gospels were composed, early in their documentary histories, or after they were widely circulating. Can we make conspiracy more credible by allowing in more coincidence?

Suppose that the writer of John's Gospel, or perhaps an early editor or copyist, noticed that the sign on the cross presented an opportunity. Not only was this person aware of the existence of Matthew, Mark, and Luke, but they also anticipated the future sacred status of those gospels. They saw that the sign on the cross proclaimed Jesus as the Messiah. Finally, they noticed that three languages in which the inscription could have been written were capable of representing previous narratives.

To recognize such an opportunity would require astounding insight at a time as early as the publication of the Fourth Gospel, which can be dated no later than AD 150. Around the middle of the second century, Justin Martyr makes a likely reference to material from John.[42] Our oldest fragment of any gospel manuscript (labeled P52) is a small scrap of papyrus containing parts of five verses from John chapter 18 (vv. 31–33, 37–38) and is dated to the mid-second century or earlier.

Even if we grant that someone had the genius to incorporate the hologram into the Fourth Gospel, the theory of opportunistic creation fails to clear the hurdle of plausibility. It might occur to an author that a sign carrying a legal charge could serve a symbolic function, but it was Mark who first placed the sign in the crucifixion scene, not the author of John.

We must also consider the small variations in the sign that mirror the differences among the Synoptics and predate John. Add further the exegetical proofs that the sign qualifies as a written gospel, most of which likewise occur in the Synoptics and were beyond the control of the

---

42 See Justin Martyr, *First Apology* 61 (cf. John 3:3); less definitely, language from John's Gospel (5:19; 16:28; 1:1; 8:29) is echoed in the *Letter of Ignatius to the Magnesians* (7.1–2; 8.2) which dates to the middle of the second century or earlier.

Fourth Evangelist. Even if the Synoptics were established as fixtures of Christian tradition before John's Gospel was composed, is it likely that their number and character would allow them to be represented by the languages in which the crucifixion charge could have been written?

Of the languages of first-century Palestine, Aramaic seems to have been the vernacular of most of the Jewish population. Hebrew was the language of worship, at least for Scripture readings in synagogues, and may have been spoken in some Judean villages. Greek, the language of the world at large, was spoken by Gentile residents and a minority of Jews, including wealthy merchants, aristocrats, and Jews who had spent time outside of their homeland. Latin was spoken among Roman officers and officials.

The writer or editor of John's Gospel had just three names available for these four key languages because, as we noted in Chapter 4, the term "Hebrew" in John embraces the dialect of Aramaic typically spoken by first-century Judeans. The language names that were both available to the editor of the Fourth Gospel and historically plausible to incorporate into the sign on the cross were precisely those suited to represent the Synoptic trio. If a contributor to John consciously chose to create the hologram, it was because against astronomical odds all the requisite materials were laid out and waiting for them.

Even if collusion and contrivance have failed us as explanations, need we resort to divine inspiration? We are bound to stumble upon coincidences, even amazingly unlikely ones, in literature and life in general. Someone picks the winning number in the lottery. A dinner plate shatters on the floor, and one of the pieces looks uncannily like the profile of Abraham Lincoln. One other consideration, however, can help to separate a statistical fluke from a product of purpose: the purposeful creation makes sense in its context. How does the hologram fare by that standard?

Far from being merely novel, the hologram appears to have a prophetic function. Assuming there actually was a sign on the cross in three languages, it foreshadowed the three-sided testimony of the Synoptic Gospels. The preservation of the key to the sign's full meaning only in the Fourth Gospel served to link it firmly to the Synoptics. Even if we discount the sign as historical fact and view it strictly in literary terms, it is the kind of unifying symbolic detail that a human author might employ when composing a single work in four parts.

The hologram makes yet more sense if it is not a unique phenomenon in the Bible. It is important, therefore, that in the Old Testament we encounter other miniature depictions. One is the Ark of the Covenant, the sacred wooden chest which contained the tablets of the testimony and which was housed in Yahweh's temple. On top of the chest, at either end, were sculptures of *cherubim*, guarding angels. The ark symbolized the transcendent abode of God, where legions of angels attend him to carry out his will.

The Ark of the Covenant's means of transport is one of its subtle prophetic features. The Ark was carried by priests like a litter with wooden poles extending through rings attached to the corners (Exod 25:12–15). When the building of the first Jerusalem temple was completed, the Ark was moved from the portable enclosure, the tabernacle, to its new resting place. The Ark was screened off in a relatively small chamber at the temple's center, the Most Holy compartment. To fit the Ark into the room reserved for it, the carrying poles were shifted forward so that they were prominently visible either to the high priest as he approached the Ark or to the priests who served in the adjoining holy space (1 Kings 8:1–9; 2 Chron 5:2–10).

The Ark was lost to history at the time of the Babylonian conquest, but when the Jews returned from exile, a practice began of publicly reading the Torah scroll as described in the books of Ezra and Nehemiah. As the people watched the priest read from the Law of Moses, they would see the upper wooden spindles of the scroll, resembling the wooden poles that had projected from the Ark's resting place. They would be reminded that behind the spindles was the sacred repository of the words of God, offering them a glimpse of his majesty and holiness.

6

Prophetic Miniatures

It is clear that representative models and prophetic tokens are not foreign to the Bible. We are specifically looking for inscribed symbols, like the sign on the cross.

The Old Testament tells us about an object called the breastplate of judgment, which under certain circumstances could be used to request a solemn decision from Yahweh. Otherwise, the Jewish high priest wore it as a badge of his office. Attached to the breastplate were sixteen sacred stones. Two of these, the Urim and Thummim, the stones for inquiry of Yahweh, were concealed in pockets or pouches. Two others were attached to the tops of the shoulder straps like epaulets, each inscribed with six of the names of the twelve sons of Jacob (Exod 28:4–41).

The remaining twelve were mounted across the front in four rows of three stones each. These front-facing stones were also engraved, each with one of the names of the sons of Israel "for their twelve tribes" (Exod 28:21; 39:14). The stones represented the nation as a whole for which the priest ministered, but the name of one tribe of Israel must have been missing.

To understand why one name was absent from the front of the breastplate, we must briefly review some patriarchal history. The man Jacob, who was also given the name Israel, had twelve sons. Normally, the oldest son of the family would be the principal heir. When the father died, the firstborn male would become the family leader and receive a double portion of the father's property. For example, if a man had two sons, the older would receive two-thirds of the estate, and the younger, one-third (Deut 21:17). Jacob's family was exceptional in that his three oldest sons committed serious sins that disqualified each of them as principal heir.

Since the privilege of the firstborn in Jacob's family had been forfeited by his sons Reuben, Simeon, and Levi, it passed to two of the remaining sons, Judah and Joseph. Judah assumed leadership, while Joseph received a double share of the inheritance (1 Chron 5:1–2; cf. Ezek 47:13). While eleven of the sons each had one tribe or clan that would later bear his name, Joseph's family formed two tribes, named for Joseph's own two sons, Manasseh and Ephraim. The two tribes of Joseph were distinct, with separate land inheritances.

The double portion awarded to Joseph made Israel a nation of thirteen tribes instead of twelve. At the time of the exodus from Egypt, God set apart one of the tribes, Levi, to serve as priests and temple workers. The Levites were given no land inheritance in Israel, they provided no soldiers to the army, and they did not have a marching position around the camp of Israel as did the twelve; instead, Levi marched at the center. Because Levi was specially assigned, it was excluded from the twelve tribes as they were normally reckoned (Num 1:47–53; 18:20–21).

Consequently, the twelve stones of the breastplate, which were designated for the twelve tribes, would not have included the name "Levi." However, when the high priest ministered, all the tribes were represented before God inasmuch as the priest himself, who wore the breastplate, represented Levi. This arrangement is reminiscent of the way the sign on the cross in John, by representing the Synoptic Gospels, symbolically ties itself to them while remaining at a distance from them.

Another example of an inscribed model comes from the book of Ezekiel. For their idolatry and moral corruption, God allowed the devastation of both the northern and southern kingdoms of Israel. Assyria shattered the northern kingdom in the late eighth century BCE. Judah faced an onslaught by the Babylonians a little over a century later. At first the Babylonians merely demanded submission. They took a few thousand educated Jews back to Babylon but left the nation and its capital, Jerusalem, intact.

Through his prophets, God commanded the king and princes of Judah to accept Babylonian domination as a discipline from him. When they defiantly rebelled instead, God told them their doom was unavoidable. Jeremiah sounded this warning in Judah, while Ezekiel did so among the Jewish refugees in Babylon.

To portray the fate decreed upon Jerusalem, God instructed Ezekiel to pantomime the siege of the Jewish capital using a miniature model of the city. The model consisted of a common brick, as the following passage from the book of Ezekiel describes:

> "And you, O son of man, take a brick and lay it before you, and portray upon it a city, even Jerusalem; and put siegeworks against it, and build a siege wall against it, and cast up a mound against it; set camps also against it, and plant battering rams against it round about. And take an iron plate, and place it as an iron wall between you and the city; and set your face toward it, and let it be in a state of siege, and press the siege against it. This is a sign for the house of Israel." (Ezekiel 4:1–3)

The Hebrew word for "portray" in the passage above means to inscribe, usually letters and words but sometimes pictures. The besieged brick upon which Jerusalem was written or depicted would become a portent of what was coming and proof afterward that God had fulfilled his word, since false prophets among the Jews were saying that the revolt against Babylon would succeed.

Ezekiel's pantomimed siege, like the brick he inscribed, was a prophetic token of a larger reality. Back in Judah, the prophet Jeremiah put a yoke upon his shoulders to show that the yoke of Babylonian rule over the land of Israel was decreed by God (Jer 27:1–8; 28:10–14).

In earlier times, the prophets Hosea and Isaiah were commanded to perform certain actions as prophetic signs. God asked Hosea to marry a promiscuous woman to reflect the chronic unfaithfulness of the people of the northern kingdom toward Yahweh, their covenant husband and Lord (Hos 1:2). In the southern kingdom, Isaiah had to walk through

Jerusalem naked and barefoot to show that Assyria would drag away into slavery Egyptians and Ethiopians, which were peoples with whom the Israelites formed protective alliances rather than turning back to Yahweh in repentance (Isa 20:2–4).

The Deceptive Tree

Prophetic miniatures continue into the New Testament, the most familiar being the fig tree cursed by Jesus. We read in Matthew and Mark that on the morning after Jesus' arrival in Jerusalem, just days before the Passover and his crucifixion, he sees a fig tree full of leaves. Fig trees normally do not put out leaves or fruit in early spring, around the time of Passover, but later, just before summer. The tree seen by Jesus has put out its leaves early. It has the sign of fruit, but when Jesus comes looking for it, he finds none. He then says to the tree, "Let no one eat fruit from you ever again." The next day, as Jesus and the disciples pass the tree, they see that it has withered. The disciples are amazed, and Jesus explains that miracles can be performed through faith.[43]

But why did Jesus perform this uncharacteristically destructive miracle? In the gospels, we see clues that it is an acted prophecy rather than a spoken one. Jesus has come to the Jewish capital looking for the fruit of righteousness. Though professing their devotion to God—giving a promise of fruit—the priests and teachers of the law prove to be spiritually barren. Out of self-interest, they reject Jesus and conspire to kill him, and thereby doom themselves to destruction. Here is how Mark frames the first part of the narrative about the tree:

> "And he entered Jerusalem, and went into the temple; and when he had looked round at everything, as it was already late, he went out to Bethany with the twelve. On the following day, when they came from Bethany, he was hungry. And seeing in the distance a fig tree in leaf, he went to see if he could find anything on it." (Mark 11:11–13)

---

43 Matt 21:18–22; Mark 11:11–14, 20–23.

On the eve of his entry into Jerusalem, Jesus went to the spiritual heart of the nation, the temple, and inspected it. He looked around at everything. The next morning he did another inspection, this time of the fig tree. We know that he was disappointed after examining the tree. How had he felt after inspecting the temple? We don't have to guess, because immediately after Jesus curses the fruitless tree, he goes straight to the temple and drives merchants and moneychangers out of the temple courts where they've set up shop. As we discussed in Chapter 4, Jesus accused merchants at the temple of turning it into a den of thieves. He would have seen the evidence of this spiritually fruitless condition when he toured the temple the evening before he inspected the tree.

On the day when the disciples notice that the tree has withered, Jesus tells a parable at the temple about a man who plants a vineyard, rents it out to tenant farmers, then sends his servants and finally his son to collect the fruit. The evil tenants, instead of handing over the fruit, assault the servants and murder the son. As with the fig tree, the fruit of righteousness that the vineyard owner has rightfully expected is not forthcoming (Mark 12:1–8; cf. Isa 5:2, 7).

A fig tree produces figs, and a vineyard produces grapes and wine. Jesus illustrates spiritual qualities by the same combination of agricultural products. "You will know them by their fruits," he says. "Are grapes gathered from thorns, or figs from thistles?" (Matt 7:16).

Luke's Gospel lacks the saying in Matthew that combines figs and grapes. He also lacks the story in Matthew and Mark about Jesus cursing the fig tree near the Temple Mount. Instead, Luke alone records a parable of Jesus about a landowner who comes looking for fruit on a fig tree that is planted in the middle of a vineyard (Luke 13:6–9). The tree is fruitless for the third year in a row, so the owner wants it cut down. The servant of the owner asks him to wait one more year for the tree to bear fruit before removing it.

The total time of four years in the parable of the fig tree may refer to the combined lengths of the ministries of John the Baptist and Jesus. According to Matthew and Luke, John the Baptist had warned that the ax was lying at the root of the trees as a symbol of judgment (Matt 3:10;

Luke 3:9). Jesus seems to have told the parable about the fruitless fig tree during the final year of his ministry, a few months before he entered Jerusalem and cursed a real fig tree that had plenty of leaves but no fruit.

The comparison of Israel to a fruit-bearing vine, an entire vineyard, or a fig tree goes back to the Old Testament prophets.[44] "'When I would gather them,' says the LORD, 'there are no grapes on the vine, nor figs on the fig tree; even the leaves are withered, and what I gave them has passed away from them'" (Jer 8:13).

Given the setting of Jesus' cursing of the fig tree, the related sayings and parables of John the Baptist and Jesus himself, and the figures of speech used by the Old Testament prophets, there is no reasonable doubt that Jesus used the tree as a prophetic model of Israel and that his actions illustrated the inspection of the nation and its coming judgment.

Death's Acre

Like the holographic sign on the cross, our final example of a prophetic model is a feature of the crucifixion of Jesus. Back in Chapter 1, we saw that among God's promises to Israel is one that challenges not only faith but also human imagination. He declared that he would do away with death. "He will swallow up death forever," says Isaiah 25:8. The apostle Paul saw this promise as being fulfilled through Jesus, whose death in perfect obedience to God's will led to his own resurrection and will culminate in a general resurrection of all the dead and a new kind of nature where death has no place.

Paul touches on this subject in Romans chapter 8, but his greatest exposition of it is in the fifteenth chapter of 1 Corinthians. Paul quotes from Isaiah 25:8 at 1 Corinthians 15:54, as he is describing the resurrection of believers to immortal life. Earlier in that chapter, in verses 25 to 27, he relates the conquest of death to Christ's exaltation as divine king by quoting two popular passages from the Psalms. Paul says, "For he [Christ] must reign until he has put all his enemies under his feet. The

---

44 Ps 80:8–16; Isa 5:1–7; Jer 2:21; Ezek 15:1–6; 17:1–24; 19:10–14; Hos 9:10; 10:1.

last enemy to be destroyed is death. 'For God has put all things in subjection under his feet.'"

Paul initially alludes to Psalm 110:10, in which Yahweh invites the Messianic King to be enthroned at his right hand "until I make your enemies your footstool." Paul interjects that the last of the enemies to be so subdued is death, just before he quotes another psalm, Psalm 8, verse 6: "You have put all things under his feet." That psalm begins by recognizing man's insignificance in comparison to the cosmos. It goes on to praise God for nevertheless glorifying man and granting him dominion over all earthly creation. Another New Testament passage, Hebrews 2:6, says that Jesus is the only man to whom Psalm 8:6 applies. Paul interprets the verse similarly by saying that Jesus, the divine man and new "Adam," is supreme over all (1 Cor 15:25–27, 45).

To put something under one's feet, in biblical terms, is to wield power over it. To raise one's foot against someone is to attack him, and to put an enemy underfoot is to destroy him.[45] The metaphor is common in the Middle East even today. On December 14, 2008, an Iraqi reporter threw his shoes at US President George W. Bush during a press conference. The reporter was venting his contempt for US policies and for its president in particular. In the Arab world, to display the sole of your shoe is an insult, an invitation to be defeated and humiliated.

Paul says that every enemy will be under Jesus' feet, and death will be destroyed, because, he then repeats, God has put everything under his Son's feet. Death, clearly, is among the enemies brought to nothing under the feet of Christ.

Paul's language concerning the end of death through Jesus unlocks a prophetic miniature having to do with the cross, but not the cross as a jewel-encrusted talisman or an embroidered religious decoration. The cross in view here is a rough-hewn executional post. Our only skeleton of a crucified man from the first century still has a nail through one of the heel bones. The victim's feet may have been nailed through the heels on either side of the upright beam rather than through the instep, as in devotional paintings. To imagine a man unable to ease pressure on

---

45 Josh 10:4; Ps 41:9; Mal 4:3; John 13:18; Rom 16:20.

his arms and chest except by standing on nails skewering his heels is to appreciate what an ugly business crucifixion was. It was not conducive to graceful poses.

Crucifixions were meant to instill fear of Roman power, so they had to be public. At the same time, naked men nailed in grotesque postures, agonizing in their blood and body fluids, would be too incendiary inside the city of Jerusalem, so the site for regular executions would have been outside the city walls. Still, it was close enough so that passersby entering and leaving the city were unable to avoid the spectacle.

The book of Hebrews says that the crucifixion took place outside Jerusalem's gate, a detail corroborated by the gospels (Heb 13:12; Matt 28:11). Knowing where Jesus died, Matthew and Luke go so far as to alter the parable of the Vineyard and Tenants as given in Mark. Mark has the son of the story being killed and thrown out of the vineyard, whereas Matthew and Luke say he was thrown out of the vineyard and killed, thereby aligning the parable more precisely with the circumstances of Jesus' death.[46] John's Gospel agrees about the location, noting that the crucifixion site was "near the city" in the same verse that contains the inscription on the cross (John 19:20).

John further says that Jesus was put in a tomb that was close to the execution site, which made it possible to inter his body hastily before the Sabbath began at sunset. Tombs were ritually defiling to the Jews, so gravesites had to be outside Jerusalem and were often grouped together so that people could avoid them. One tomb meant others in the area, a graveyard consisting of filled trenches and, for the wealthy, tunnels chiseled into a rocky hillside where remains could be placed in niches.[47]

A rich disciple, Joseph of Arimathea, used his own newly cut tomb for the body of Jesus. Tombs were usually owned by families so that family members could be buried together. Joseph was from a district northwest of Jerusalem and apparently had no close relatives in the city where he came to make his home. This could be why the tomb was new. John says

---

46 Matt 21:39; Luke 20:15; cf. Mark 12:8.
47 For detailed information about contemporary burial practices and the location of the tomb of Jesus, see Gibson, *The Final Days of Jesus: The Archaeological Evidence* (HarperCollins, 2009).

the tomb was in a garden, an amenity for someone who could afford to adorn his future resting place.

Even the decorated corner of a cemetery conceals putrefaction. So, when the Evangelists tell us about an execution site near to pits for corpses, they are describing not so much two places as one, the home of death. And in all of the Four Gospels, this place is given a name.

While I was working on this book, I asked one of my sons, who was eleven years old at the time, "What's the universal symbol of death?" I gave him no hint of why I was asking, but he answered immediately, with a confidence that surprised me. "The skull," he said. The skull has indeed stood for death through the ages and around the world, from Mesoamerica to India.

The reason for the skull's power as a symbol is clear enough. When people find bones lying on the ground, or encounter them while digging, they are often scattered. A casual observer might have trouble distinguishing the isolated vertebrae, ribs, and limb bones of a human from those of a goat or a small deer. The human skull, on the other hand, is unmistakable. It instantly says that a human being has died. The uniqueness of the human skull is due to its huge braincase, which is a reminder that even humans' crowning glory, their intellect, succumbs to the relentless onslaught of mortality. The skull as a symbol is also known in English as the "death's head."

In the Old Testament, the Hebrew word for "skull" is used one of two ways. It has a technical use in giving tallies of people, somewhat like the term "head count" in English, that has no dark overtones. Otherwise, it occurs just three times, with connotations more like those of the English word. The three instances all have to do with violent, even grisly death: the first tells about Abimelech, a cutthroat whose murderous career ends when his skull is crushed by a millstone; the second describes the Philistines mounting the skull of Israel's first king, Saul, as a war trophy; the last tells how the body of wicked queen Jezebel is eaten by dogs who leave behind only her hands, her feet, and her skull.[48]

---

48 Judg 9:53; 2 Kgs 9:35; 1 Chron 10:10.

According to all of the Four Gospels, the crucifixion site just outside Jerusalem was known as "skull place" or "the skull," *kranion* in Greek, from which we get "cranium." In Latin, "skull" is *calveria*, hence the term Calvary that comes to us from Latin Bibles such as the Vulgate. The Aramaic word for skull is *gulgalta*; the corresponding Hebrew is *gulgoleth*. Both Aramaic and Hebrew can be heard in the dialect form *golgotha*, the word we find in Matthew, Mark, and John, in addition to *kranion*. Was there a skull-shaped landmark nearby that gave Golgotha its name? If so, it was probably obliterated long ago by building, destruction, and filling in northwest Jerusalem. Alternatively, was the place named because of the regular executions there or because of the adjoining graveyard?

Whatever the reason, the killing ground to which Jesus was led on a spring morning around the year 30 CE was named for the universal symbol of death. There he was put to death, but not lying prostrate in the dust. Jesus died above the ground by a meter or more, as indicated by clues scattered across the gospels. In Matthew and Mark, Jesus' opponents mockingly invite him to "come down" from the cross. When pangs of thirst cause Jesus to cry out, the soldiers wonder aloud if Elijah will come and "take him down," according to Mark. Then, according to Matthew, Mark, and John, they put a sponge on the end of a stick to give him a sip of vinegar, presumably because of his height above the ground. Finally, after his death, Joseph of Arimathea "takes him down" from the cross for burial.[49]

Jesus died in an upright posture above the bloody patch of earth that is named as death's territory. Death was, as it were, put under his feet. Regardless of the dramatic symbolism that seems to be at work here, the fate of Jesus appeared to be a victory for death. But the Bible claims that far from merely dying, Jesus suffered in perfect obedience to the will of God the Father, something no human had ever done (Phil 2:8). Even the phrase "perfect obedience" implies death, insofar as "perfect" in the Hebrew conception means "complete," and to be complete, obedience must be exhaustively tested.

---

49 Matt 27:40, 42, 48; Mark 15:36, 46; John 19:29; Acts 13:29.

The Son of God, the Scriptures say, came into a world that is contaminated by sin and therefore in the grip of pain and mortality. No one can enter such a world as a participant and remain untouched by the pain and death that suffuse it. Imagine a maximum security prison in which the most violent inmates have seized control. The warden cannot choose to enter the prison unarmed and expose himself to the evil there, even with the best of motives, without paying a terrible price.

Paul says that when the Son of God chose to exist as a human being, truly and fully entering this world, he humbled himself and became obedient to the point of death, even death on a cross (Phil 2:5–11). By doing so in absolute sinlessness, he morally and spiritually overcame the power of death. He laid the foundation for a future world, a new nature where, to quote Revelation, "death will be no more, neither shall there be mourning nor crying nor pain anymore" (Rev 21:3–4).

Although the circumstances of Jesus' crucifixion are well covered in the Synoptic Gospels, only in John does Jesus hint that the manner of his death will dramatically portray the cosmic victory that it entails. In the following passages, Jesus is quoted as using the term "lifted up" to describe his coming execution:

> "When you have lifted up the Son of man, then you will know that I am he, and that I do nothing on my own authority but speak thus as the Father taught me." (John 8:28)

> "I, when I am lifted up from the earth, will draw all men to myself. He said this to show by what death he was to die." (John 12:32–33)

The Greek for "lifted up" is *hypsoo*. It can mean to raise or lift up physically, as Jesus was raised up on the cross, or metaphorically to elevate or exalt. In the Septuagint Bible, the same word occurs in Isaiah 52:13: "My servant shall understand and be exalted." It is used in Acts for the exaltation of Jesus to the right hand of God after his resurrection (Acts 2:33; 5:31). In John's Gospel, the literal and figurative meanings of *hypsoo* blend. The crucifixion itself becomes a kind of exaltation, because at the cross death's power is overcome.

The King's Heralds

Features of Jesus' death that came together to represent a larger, abstract reality also function as prophecy. Two Pauline texts refer to Christ's triumph as an accomplished fact (2 Cor 2:14; Col 2:15), but when Paul says in 1 Corinthians 15 that Jesus will subdue all his enemies, among them death, he contemplates the future kingdom of God. As we have seen, these present and future aspects are both evident in John. John chapter 12's statement that the Son will draw all men when he is lifted up is reminiscent of Philippians 2:10, where Paul says that in the coming world every knee will bow to Jesus. Jesus conquered at the cross, but the full results lie in the future.

Even the garden at the entrance to Jesus' tomb, which seemed a vain attempt to beautify corruption, in the light of atonement is transformed into a token of paradise beyond the grave. Just as God, according to Genesis, finished his work and then rested on the seventh day, Jesus, after finishing his own work, rested in the garden tomb on the Sabbath. If the gospels are to be believed, the darkness of the tomb was soon pierced by the light of resurrection life so that, as Isaiah had predicted, the Messiah's resting place became glorious (Mark 16:4–6; Isa 11:10).

Let's revisit Paul's declaration, in 1 Corinthians 15, that Jesus will reign until every enemy is vanquished. In English, the words "king" and "reign" are dissimilar because "king" is from Old Germanic and "reign" is from Latin. Such is not the case in biblical Greek, where the words "king," *basileus*, and "reign," *basileuo*, are cognate. To bring this connection into English, we could translate Paul as saying that Jesus must be king until every enemy is beneath his feet, including the last enemy, death.

At the crucifixion, death—Golgotha—is underneath the feet not just of Jesus, the Galilean rabbi, but of Jesus reigning. That is evident from an object we have already devoted much attention to, the sign over Jesus' head whose words are often abbreviated as INRI for the Latin *Iesus Nazarenus Rex Iudaeorum,* "Jesus the Nazarene, the King of the Jews." The elements of the crucifixion scene combine to herald Jesus as king over death, death's conqueror and destroyer.

We have now come full circle, in the process having established that the gospel hologram makes sense in the context of the Bible as a whole. Besides prophetic models in the Old Testament, we looked at the New Testament examples of the cursing of the fig tree and the exaltation of Jesus over death at the crucifixion. Those willing to search for other examples can locate them. The Fourth Gospel's encoding of the tripartite Synoptic canon is unusual only because it unambiguously defies natural explanation.

Symbolism of the kind we have reviewed makes sense in literary as well as spiritual terms. Convergence of form and content unifies a work of literature and reinforces its ideas. Consider as a simple example the word "staccato." It means a series of sounds that are sharp and distinct from one another, like the rat-a-tat of a machine gun. With its clipped syllables, *staccato* has the same characteristic it describes. The word gains expressive power from the combination of form and content. Likewise, as we've just considered, the way Jesus died coincides with his death's significance.

Layered meaning is a device so common in literature that we could sift examples endlessly. Let's consider one from Shakespeare's play, *Hamlet*. In it, the young prince Hamlet of Denmark becomes suspicious that the present king, his uncle, murdered Hamlet's father, the former king, in order to gain the throne. Hamlet arranges for his uncle to watch a play in which an assassin murders a king by pouring poison into the king's ear as he sleeps. Hamlet hopes to provoke a guilty reaction in his uncle.

As the play begins, Hamlet mockingly assures his uncle that the evil they see portrayed ought not to faze people like themselves. However, the assassin in the play is the nephew of the king he kills. In the course of trying to depict his uncle's wickedness onstage, Hamlet recreates himself as well. Hamlet pours verbal poison into the ear of his uncle, the king, shortly before the nephew in the play pours liquid poison into the ear of his uncle, the onstage king.

Shakespeare's play-within-a-play becomes a hall of mirrors. It even implies that we, the audience of the larger play, *Hamlet*, might glimpse ourselves onstage. Perhaps there is more resemblance than we care to admit between each of us and the title character, who struggles toward truth amid uncertainty and wrestles with his own flawed character.

The layered meaning of *Hamlet* is strictly suggestive and resulted from the creative genius of a single author. The multi-faceted meaning of the gospel hologram, though more objectively evidenced, cuts across the work of several independent authors. The doctrine of the inspiration of Scripture says that God guided the writers without erasing their personalities, so that their genuinely human expressions are backlit by God's thoughts.

The doctrine of inspiration has a corollary, which is that God imperceptibly superintended the historical circumstances and countless human choices that gave us Scripture as a divine library. He made sure that remaining uncertainties about the text of the Bible are insufficient to obscure the spiritual truth it contains.

Winnowing the Oracle

Even if we view the gospel hologram as evidence of the divine orchestration of events, we must also acknowledge that evidence requires interpretation. A virtue of the scientific process is that it narrows the range for reasonable interpretation of facts. The Bible illustrates the benefit of controlling the way facts are construed. In a story in the book of Daniel, King Nebuchadnezzar II of Babylon has a dream and wants to know what it means. Like his contemporaries, he assumes that dreams are omens if interpreted correctly. The king's wise men are eager to give him their opinion, but the king declines to tell them what occurred in the dream. Instead, the king asks them to relate his dream back to him before they explain its meaning (Dan 2:1–11).

Is the story implying that Nebuchadnezzar had forgotten the dream? Or instead, does the king realize that relating the dream back to him as he remembers it would be a more impressive demonstration of his wise men's powers than their being able to spin an interpretation? His motive is unclear, but his method illustrates the way careful observation and close analysis minimize interpretive fuzziness.

In the story, Nebuchadnezzar's test succeeds in separating the one true prophet, Daniel, from the crowd of conjurers and soothsayers who lack supernatural information. In this book, I have endeavored to distinguish its subject from sensational religious claims.[50] We have discovered a remarkable coordinating linkage among the gospels based on close study and careful definitions. The available information points away from the possibility that human effort created this linkage during the writing, editing, reception, or compilation of the gospels. Finally, Scripture's implicit claim of divine inspiration provides an internal rationale for what I have called the "gospel hologram."

---

50 An example may be veneration of the "Titulus Crucis," a relic supposed by some to be the original wooden plaque from the cross, now housed in the Cappella delle Reliquie in Rome and radiocarbon dated to the Middle Ages.

7

Faith Versus Reason?

Perhaps someone will take up the challenge to look outside the Bible for an apparent convergence of symbols, concepts, and narrative details like those of the gospel hologram. The counterexample must be equally well-defined. The non-biblical "hologram" must amplify a theme spanning different documents that have different authors, circumstances of composition, and writing styles. Finally, the body of literature in which it occurs must contain an internal explanation corresponding to inspiration and the divine ordering of history. If an observer can locate such a multi-level representation, then the gospel hologram will no longer command as much of our attention. However, the likelihood of their doing so is slim.

Bart Ehrman, whose work we have noted, argues in his book *Jesus, Interrupted* that a natural explanation of events will always be more likely than one that is supernatural or miraculous. If the odds are one in a million that the Evangelists colluded to create the hologram, or one in ten million that it arose by sheer chance, the odds are even smaller that divine inspiration produced it. The reason is that, according to Ehrman, a miracle is by definition the least likely explanation for any set of facts.[51]

---

51 Ehrman, *Jesus Interrupted*, 172–179.

Ehrman offers us a rule for interpreting evidence disguised as a con-clusion based on the evidence. If we take him seriously, a natural expla-nation must be assumed under any conceivable circumstance. For example, if thousands of diverse, otherwise normal people heard a voice speak to them out of a clear sky, it would be more plausibly ex-plained as a collective auditory hallucination than as something other-worldly. If so, what evidence of the miraculous could God provide?

We can trace Ehrman's line of reasoning back to the eighteenth-cen-tury Scottish philosopher David Hume. In an essay on miracles in his book, *An Enquiry Concerning Human Understanding*, Hume points out that people are fascinated by wonders and the supernatural, and they are prone to believing uncritically in miracles that confirm their own religious convictions. On the other hand, we all doubt miracles in reli-gions other than our own.

Considering that human beings are prone to dishonesty, exaggera-tion, mistakes, and misjudgments, Hume argues, the report of an event that defies the laws of nature is always better explained by some form of human fallibility than by action on the part of God or other invisible agents.[52]

Hume was correct that we have reason to be cautious in evaluating claims about the supernatural, but he took this caution too far when he made it a rule for interpreting evidence. That final move is fatal to his argument because such a rule cannot itself be tested against the evi-dence.

In biblical terms, some events appear to reflect God's purpose in an obvious way. We call these events miracles when we cannot attribute their apparently purposeful character to human foresight or intention. For example, to predict a severe drought, as Elijah is claimed to have done in the Old Testament, would qualify as a miracle (1 Kings 17:1). Compare the prediction that Babylonian armies would destroy Jerusalem in the sixth century BCE. The Babylonian attack fulfilled God's warning, expressed through prophets such as Jeremiah, that he

---

52 David Hume, *An Enquiry Concerning Human Understanding* (1748), Section X, "Of Miracles."

would punish Judah for its corruption (Jer 5:14–17). However, the prediction need not have been supernatural, insofar as the prophets might reasonably have foreseen Babylon's response to Judah's duplicity.

Miracles may appear to defy the laws of nature, as when Jesus turned water into wine and walked on the waves of the Sea of Galilee (John 2:1–10; 6:16–21). Alternatively, they may not. Unusually large catches of fish, such as those described in Luke chapter 5 and John chapter 21, do not violate the laws of nature. But the occurrence of those events immediately after Jesus instructed the disciples to cast their nets qualifies them as miraculous.

In the case of the miracles recorded in the gospels, we have no detailed outside corroboration. Believing those events to be historical requires us to trust the Evangelists as faithful recorders of what they either observed or learned from others. In the preface to Luke's Gospel, the writer reveals that he is not himself an eyewitness of Jesus' ministry, and he implicitly asks us to rely on his judgment regarding unnamed sources.

The gospels' credibility benefits from their literary and spiritual power and from substantial accuracy in historical details of time and place. Some of the miracles they describe have parallels in non-biblical literature of the same period, but these are what people of the time would expect as demonstrations of divine empowerment (John 4:48).

What is of central importance is the way Jesus, in his words and works, in his life and death, addresses and expands on the promising yet tortured story of Israel, and the way that enlarged story in turn addresses the cosmic discomfort of human beings and their longing for union with the divine. To put this information in perspective requires us to make spiritual judgments, but along the way we may glimpse tokens of divine action such as we have considered in this book.

Even if we speculate that Jesus of Nazareth never lived and that the Four Gospels are purely legendary, to the extent that the hologram resists explanation in natural terms, it is miraculous. More precisely, the literary and historical data combine to cast doubt on natural explanations. Moreover, the hologram is just one prophetic alignment out of many that are present in the Bible but absent from collections of non-biblical literature.[53]

Some secularists, rather than ruling out any and all indications of supernatural activity, have adopted the more reasonable position that extraordinary claims require extraordinary evidence. But weighing beliefs against experience can cut in more than one direction. Ordinary explanations cannot be maintained when extraordinary evidence makes its entrance.

Faith on the Defensive

Although faith can coexist with reason, too many believers have minimized the connection between the two. They feel that what the Bible calls "human wisdom" is not just reasoning that seeks to exclude God but almost any logical reasoning on spiritual matters. A balanced reading of Scripture does not support such a rejection, but it is a common reaction against the intellectual revolution begun in the seventeenth century by French thinker Rene Descartes, among others, that has come to be called the Enlightenment. The Enlightenment saw the flowering of science and vigorous debate over ideas, including religious beliefs. Skeptics challenged the Christian faith, and secularism gained a following that has increased over time.

The architects of the Enlightenment prioritized evidence and rational argument over tradition and authority. Descartes, who recommended reason and experiment as means to truth, said that for him faith held a privileged position.[54] Nevertheless, the categories of "evidence" and "argument" are not synonymous with the Bible and the church. One might even identify the Bible and the church with what the Enlightenment called into question—tradition and authority.

---

53 For further examples, see Barefoot, *Gospel Mysteries* (Grandling Valley Press, 2009).

54 Rene Descartes, *Discourse on the Method for Rightly Conducting One's Reason and of Seeking Truth in the Sciences* (1637), Part 3. After listing three practical maxims for living while he sought greater knowledge, Descartes says that he assigned them a protected place "along with the truths of the faith, which have always been primary among my beliefs."

Descartes struggled to keep the language of his philosophical works within the bounds prescribed by the Holy See of the Roman Catholic Church. This was especially challenging when it came to describing Earth's motion after Galileo was arrested for arguing that it orbited the sun. Descartes knew that Galileo was correct, but he fudged his language on the subject to avoid controversy. University students influenced by Descartes grew impatient with such pretenses.

Some Christians avoided the Enlightenment's intellectual battlefield. They either withdrew into private piety or took up positions on the sidelines where they could hector their opponents from a distance. That strategy has proven to be short-sighted.

The Enlightenment made room for skeptical opinion because it made possible a wider exchange of viewpoints, a situation any preacher of the gospel should relish. During the Middle Ages and Renaissance, faith was governed by the dictum *cuius regio eius religio*: the religion of the ruler is that of the realm. Freedom of speech and of religion were scarce commodities. Fitfully, at first, the Enlightenment saw the spread of these freedoms. Most of the Christians alive today who look back on the Enlightenment with disdain would have been imprisoned, tortured, exiled, or executed as religious rebels had they lived before Enlightenment ideals took hold.

By the end, in 1648, of Europe's Thirty Years' War, during which armies across the continent slaughtered each other in the name of Christ, enthusiasm for violent suppression of ideas (at least of religious ideas) was waning. Wherever tolerance gained ground, it spawned both defiance and defense of Christian faith.

The Enlightenment also owed to a pair of events that had taken place, respectively, in the early fifteenth and early sixteenth centuries. The first was the invention of the printing press. The second was the Protestant Reformation, which challenged the authority of the Roman Catholic Church. Martin Luther and other reformers championed the Bible and promoted its distribution to a lay readership, which printing had made possible.

Clinging to the Bible while doubting church teachings implied a question. Ordinary people had accepted the Bible—a book that for centuries they had only heard from the pulpit, in Latin—as sacred truth on the authority of the church. How could the Bible be trusted as a record of the apostolic faith if church authority were called into question? Careful comparison of manuscripts and the study of their history might bolster its credibility. Thinkers marshaled the Enlightenment's methods to recommend, as well as to question, the Scriptures.

The Roman Catholic Church, unable to contain the Reformation by force, sought any means available to defend its position. It urged its theologians to debate the Reformers and write books answering their charges. The Church was itself forced to fall back on evidence and argument to buttress its authority.

As literacy spread and Bibles became available to the general public, ordinary readers could see that the New Testament is far from averse to evidence and logical reasoning. In Mark's Gospel, Jesus forgives a young paralytic of his sins, then provides evidence of his authority to do so by healing the young man of his paralysis (Mark 2:9–11). Jesus likewise points to his power to free possessed individuals from demonic control as evidence that he is truly the agent of the kingdom of God (Matt 12:24–29).

In John's Gospel, Jesus unambiguously endorses evidence as a basis for belief: "If I am not doing the works of my Father, then do not believe me; but if I do them, even though you do not believe me, believe the works, that you may know and understand that the Father is in me and I am in the Father." (John 10:37–38).

According to the book of Acts, the apostle Paul made arguments from Israel's Scriptures to Jewish audiences (Acts 18:28). When he addressed pagan Greeks in Athens, he instead appealed to the generally accepted idea of a Sovereign Creator and made a logical argument for God's transcendence (Acts 17:22–29). When Paul wrote to the church in Corinth concerning the resurrection, he noted that there were many living witnesses to the risen Jesus (1 Cor 15:6).

The New Testament is strewn with citations of evidence and invitations to reason toward sound conclusions. The Bible does not dismiss tradition and authority, but neither could proponents of the Enlightenment. At best, we can merely shift the balance among evidence, argument, authority, and tradition. Authority is indispensable to modern science, for example, unless we expect every scientist to personally conduct all experiments and make all observations pertaining to their field of study. Authority, along with tradition, provides a framework for preserving knowledge so that it can be built upon and corrected.

The emphasis on evidence and argument, harmless to the Bible in itself, became identified with the claim of David Hume, a giant of the Enlightenment, that there never could be evidence for a supernatural event; only natural causes may be entertained. Despite the flaw in Hume's reasoning that we have already noted, numerous scholars enthusiastically imported Hume's naturalism into biblical studies, in particular into the study of the New Testament Gospels. Key figures in this development were Hermann Samuel Reimarus and Gotthold Ephraim Lessing in the eighteenth century, and in the following century, David Friedrich Strauss and Joseph Ernest Renan.

Thoroughgoing naturalism became the foundation of academic biblical studies from the nineteenth century onward. Its practitioners sometimes stipulated that miracles are impossible to disprove, even though natural explanations are always preferable. Belief in anything supernatural would be a matter of faith, where faith means believing, not because of the evidence, but in spite of it.[55]

Many ordinary Christians, recoiling from the more extreme conclusions of historical criticism, unwittingly succumbed to the definition of faith as invariably the blind variety. Gotthold Lessing argued that religious convictions are assured truths of reason, but beliefs based on historical evidence are subject to revision and even rejection as more evidence comes to light.[56] He therefore presented believers with a

---

55 Hume, *op. cit.*, Section X, Part 2.
56 G.H. Lessing, "On the Proof of the Spirit and the Power" (1777).

dilemma. To refer to evidence as a basis for faith would be to admit that it was insecure.

From the nineteenth century onward, Christian leaders divided into different camps over the results of archaeology, ancient history, geology, evolutionary biology, and related areas of study. Gradually increasing numbers of them reflexively denied the results of systematic research.

Up to the present, ordinary believers have tended to remain ignorant of, and indifferent to, the range of evidence pertaining to the Bible. Too many Christians today dispute scientific findings without bothering to inform themselves adequately, yet they will repeat transparent false-hoods such as the claim that chariot wheels have been found at the bottom of the Red Sea.

Academic study, for its part, is necessarily confined to the arena of natural causes, but it does not define the boundaries of rational thought about spiritual matters. Before we conclude that what we've been studying has no importance to faith, let's revisit the dilemma proposed by Gotthold Lessing.

You Bet Your Life?

The Old Testament recommends evidence as a basis for belief, for example, in Deuteronomy 4:32–39. It also encourages rational thinking, as in the famous invitation of Isaiah 1:18, "Come, now, let us reason together." Evidence and argument, therefore, are among the means by which God's Spirit reveals truth. God also reveals himself through conscience and spiritual intuition, which are internal ways of knowing.

The evidence with which science is concerned is external. We gather it directly through our five senses or indirectly with instruments. We might call this activity *inspection.* When we look out the window to see if it is cloudy or sunny, smell a freshly cut lemon, or look at a ther-mometer to learn the exact temperature we are inspecting the world around us.

Inspection is only one route to knowledge. When someone thinks re-flectively or ponders the deeper meaning of information, they are en-gaging instead in *introspection.* The apostle Paul said that he learned by inner experience that his actions often fell short of being morally upright. "For I delight in the law of God, in my inmost self," he says in Romans 7:22–23, "but I see in my members another law at war with the law of my mind and making me captive to the law of sin which dwells in my members."

Paul realized introspectively that sin was at work in his personality. As another example, in 1 Corinthians, chapter 2, verse 11, Paul asks, "For who knows someone's thoughts except the spirit of the person which is in them?" "Spirit" in this verse means "mind." We know our thoughts not by inspection with our senses but through introspection, our inner experience of the thought process.

We weave the fabric of knowledge from the threads of both inspection and introspection. According to the Bible, God's Holy Spirit can work within the mysterious inner world of the mind and heart to shed light on external evidence, producing a conviction of faith that goes beyond mere likelihood. Forces other than God's Spirit, including biases, superstitions, and delusions, can also generate beliefs.

Gotthold Lessing suggested that we put our lives on the line, or at the least the direction of our lives, every time we weigh a new fact concerning divine revelation. If faith is so fragile, perhaps it dares not risk grappling with evidence.

Must we wager our deepest convictions just to confront new information honestly? Even though a single surprising discovery can turn a person's mind in a new direction, it rarely warrants a comprehensive change of outlook. A shift of that magnitude usually requires reflection and a variety of evidence.

In addition, faith is subject to a principle invoked by the first-century rabbi Gamaliel when he advised the Jewish Sanhedrin not to kill the apostles (Acts 5:38–39). If the mission of the apostles were just the work of men it would fail, Gamaliel argued, but if it were more than that, no one could overthrow it, and those who tried to do so would be fighting against God himself.

Gamaliel may have been applying the words of Psalm 127, "Unless the LORD builds the house, those who build it labor in vain. Unless the

LORD watches over the city, the watchman stays awake in vain" (Ps 127:1). A believer need only commit to weigh evidence fairly, not to abandon their spiritual convictions in case the evidence is challenging. In time, a fair consideration of the facts ought to be enough to sweep aside faith that is error in disguise.

If a believer's faith is genuine, then eventually God will supply them with further evidence or a clearer understanding that leaves their core convictions intact. In dialogue over matters of faith, thoughtful Christians can expect no more of unbelievers than that they consider evidence seriously when it is respectfully presented. In due course, the truth will make itself known (2 Cor 4:2; 1 Pet 3:15).

No one on any side of a discussion needs to respond when an opponent resorts to bluster, insolence, or insult. Until an argument is presented on its merits, without being accompanied by offensive language, we should avoid responding to it.

When considering historical evidence touching on the Bible, believers should also keep in mind the ways God speaks in revelation. The Bible sometimes conveys information in a stylized or idealized manner. Facts may be simplified, abbreviated, and given a particular emphasis, unlike in journalistic reporting. We've seen that the gospels sometimes paraphrase Jesus, keeping the main idea but varying his words to suit a particular Evangelist's perspective.

An example of stylized narrative is found in Luke's Gospel. Chapter 24, verses 33–51, recounts the appearance of Jesus to his disciples on the night after his resurrection. Jesus promises the disciples the Holy Spirit, then leads them out of Jerusalem and ascends to heaven in front of them. The entire sequence seems to occur one evening and the following morning. In the first chapter of Acts, the same author, Luke, reveals that Jesus appeared many times over the course of more than a month before his ascension (Acts 1:1–3).

At the end of his gospel, Luke has telescoped what happened over several weeks into one event spanning a night and a day. The scene conveys key facts, but it does not represent time with journalistic accuracy.

Thanks to such examples as this, we know it is possible that elsewhere in the Bible long sequences of events are compressed.

Luke reveals another type of stylization in Acts 7:16, which says that Abraham purchased the site of the tomb of Joseph in Shechem, northern Israel. Genesis reveals that Abraham did not personally buy that plot of land. God promised the whole land of Canaan to Abraham's descendants in future generations, but he did not permit Abraham to own land there himself. The only exception was Abraham's purchase of a burial plot for his wife and himself at Hebron, in southern Canaan (Gen 23:3–20).

Later, Abraham's grandson Jacob bought land in northern Canaan, at Shechem, for burials (Gen 33:19; Josh 24:32). Even taking the various texts at face value, we are left to conclude that Acts credits Abraham representatively with a purchase actually made by his grandson Jacob.

We find the same stylization in the books of 1 and 2 Kings in the Old Testament. Elijah was told by God to go and anoint new kings for northern Israel and Syria, but the anointing was actually performed years later by Elijah's successor, Elisha, who inherited Elijah's authority.[57]

Stylized attribution is important when we ask, for instance, who wrote the first five books of the Bible. The evidence of composite authorship over time is impressive, although exactly how this occurred entails questions incapable of definite answers. Biblical attribution is sufficiently flexible that statements about Moses' authorship require only that a Moses-like figure stands somewhere behind the tradition that produced the Pentateuch.

The principle that much is required of those to whom much is given has an implication for our present age (Luke 12:48b). Interpreting, applying, and defending Scriptural revelation has become challenging in proportion to the wealth of human knowledge, both scientific and historical, granted to recent generations. Believers are called to meet that challenge with care and discernment rather than retreating into willful ignorance.

---

57 1 Kgs 19:15–16; cf. 2 Kgs 8:8–15; 9:1–6.

The Manifold Witness

Because much of the Bible is narrative, the findings of archaeology and other historical sciences are relevant to its study. At a minimum, they show that the Bible is significantly grounded in real places, peoples, and cultures. The Bible is not largely fiction, as are the Odyssey and the Book of Mormon.

However, as we have just seen, the Bible does not always speak in ways we expect. In some cases, approximation, abbreviation, hyperbole, and idealized summaries are evident, and they could be present less obviously in other places. The Bible's narratives are, to varying degrees, history presented with a figurative slant for spiritual purposes.

Therefore, despite their value, the historical sciences cannot settle the question of the divine inspiration of the Bible. For ordinary Christians, it is the spiritual message of Scripture in its totality, with the self-sacrificing love of Jesus Christ as its focal point, that speaks most persuasively. The broad sweep of salvation history drew the attention of truth-seekers from the beginning, and not only those who were Jews.

We might have assumed until now that of the people who passed by the grisly spectacle outside a northwest gate of Jerusalem on that spring day two millennia ago, only the native inhabitants had reason to pause at the sign tacked above a dying prisoner, which declared him to be "The King of the Jews." Historical testimony offers us reason to think otherwise.

Three-and-a-half centuries before the time of Jesus, the conquests of Alexander the Great had instituted a universal language, Greek, throughout the Mediterranean world. Jews living outside the land of Israel, from Europe to Asia Minor to Egypt, had not only learned Greek but also created a Greek version of the Hebrew Bible. By the early first century, numbers of Gentiles across the Roman Empire had become acquainted with the religion of Israel. They had heard the proclamation of one God and of a savior-king who would one day appear among the people of Judah.

The prophecy of a coming Jewish king had enough currency that the Roman authorities made use of it. In his book, *The Purpose of Mark's*

Gospel: An Early Christian Response to Roman Imperial Propaganda, scholar Adam Winn cites three historians of the period: Tacitus, Suetonius, and Josephus.[58] Each of them refers to a common belief in the first century that a man or men from Judea would rule the world. They all applied this prophecy to the Emperor Vespasian or to Vespasian and his son Titus.[59]

Vespasian had taken Roman legions to Judea to put down the First Jewish Revolt, but as a result of the power vacuum left by Caesar Nero's assassination, Vespasian returned to Rome. While he secured the imperial throne, Vespasian put the army under the command of his son, Titus, who completed the conquest of Judea and became Caesar himself when Vespasian died. Because this father-and-son duo had campaigned in Judea and then become rulers of the greatest empire the world had yet known, their propagandists claimed that they had fulfilled the promise about a supreme king coming out of the land of Judah.

To anyone who had heard that a mighty king would arise in the land of the Jews, the title above the crucified construction worker-turned-rabbi would at first appear to be a cruel joke. Within a few days, according to the earliest Christian writings, Jesus' followers were claiming to have seen him alive again, not as a disembodied spirit but as a tangible human being who was now living on a higher level of reality. Strangely, the title began to make sense.

In an account in the book of Isaiah, God, through his prophet, invites King Ahaz of Israel to ask for a sign as deep as the grave or as high as the heights (Isa 7:11). Ahaz wisely declines, but the wording of God's proposal contains a clue. The greatest sign of all must stretch between height and depth, as we are told Christ did when he descended from the pinnacle of divinity to the material world on down to the bottomless blackness of the grave—and then returned. What possession of any king could surpass the power to descend to the nadir of human despair, confront death's veneer of finality, and turn the void inside out?

---

58 Josephus was Jewish, but he wrote his histories under Roman patronage.
59 See Winn, *The Purpose of Mark's Gospel*, 157–167.

Prior to Jesus, there had been myths of heroes fathered and protected by the gods. The myths intruded into history when the lives of kings and emperors were recounted. The Greek historian Herodotus tells how Cyrus the Great of Persia, shortly after his birth, was miraculously delivered from the wrath of evil King Astyages of Media.[60]

Plutarch relates that Olympias, the mother of Alexander the Great, was given an omen in a dream around the time of his conception, and that Alexander's father, Philip II of Macedon, suspected that his wife had become pregnant by supernatural means.[61] Suetonius claims that Emperor Vespasian performed at least two miraculous healings. He also reports that a comet seen after Julius Caesar's death was taken as evidence that he had been deified in the heavens. Julius's successor, Augustus, was also claimed to have ascended heavenward after his death.[62]

Pulled by people's longing for a savior and pushed by ambition and pretense, the human imagination had generated a profile of divinity. The trouble was, making human rulers out to be divine was a desperate and cynical enterprise. Numerius Atticus, the senator who swore that he saw Augustus's soul fly up to heaven from his funeral pyre, was well paid for doing so by Augustus's widow, Livia, according to the historian Cassius Dio.[63] And what about Vespasian, the emperor with the healing touch who supposedly fulfilled the prophecies about a world ruler coming from Judea? Suetonius says that when Vespasian lay on his deathbed he remarked with grim irony, "Alas, I suppose I am becoming a god."[64]

According to the gospels, most of those around God's Son misunderstood or scorned him when he displayed the signs of divinity. The title of divine kingship that the crowd bestowed upon emperors proved to be a mockery, while the title given to Jesus in mockery proved to be a glorious fact.

---

60 Herodotus, *Histories*, 1.107–121.
61 Plutarch, *Lives: Alexander.*
62 Suetonius, *The Life of Vespasian* 7.2.; *The Life of Julius Caesar* 88; *The Life of Augustus* 100.4.
63 Cassius Dio, *Roman History* 56.46.2.
64 Suetonius, *Vespasian* 23.4.

The plaque that bore witness to the Lord of the universe, who to rescue his creation was willing to be rejected, vilified, spat upon, and hung up to die, continues to testify in new ways even today.[65] If you are a believer, I hope that our exploration of the gospel hologram has deepened your appreciation of God's revelation of himself in the Scriptures. If you are not, may it move you in the direction of faith. Please remember that the truth is not simply a body of facts to be acknowledged; rather, it is the bedrock of reality, who beckons us to hear, follow, and live. "The words I have spoken to you," he tells us, "are spirit and they are life" (John 6:63).

---

65 Additional evidence of the affiliations of the Synoptic Gospels with the languages of the inscription posted on the cross will be available at the website Typologetics.com during 2026.

Scripture Index

Subject Index

Bibliography

Barefoot, Darek. *Gospel Mysteries: Typological Coding as Evidence of the Bible's Inspiration* (Grand Junction, CO: Grand Valley Press, 2009).

Beal, Timothy. *The Rise and Fall of the Bible: The Unexpected History of an Accidental Book* (New York: Houghton Mifflin Harcourt, 2011).

Bratcher, Robert. *Old Testament Quotations in the New Testament* (*Helps for Translators*) (NY: United Bible Societies, 1987) 1–27.

Descartes, Rene. *Discourse on the Method for Rightly Conducting One's Reason and of Seeking Truth in the Sciences* (1637), Part 3.

Ehrman. Bart. *Jesus, Interrupted: Revealing the Hidden Contradictions in the Bible (and Why We Don't Know About Them)* (New York: HarperCollins, 2009).

Evans, Craig. "Mark's Incipit and the Priene Calendar Inscription: From Jewish Gospel to Greco-Roman Gospel" *Journal of Greco-Roman Christianity and Judaism* 1 (2000) 67–81.

_____. "Jewish Versions of the Gospel of Matthew," *Mishkan* 38 (2003) 70–79.

Gibson, Shimon. *The Final Days of Jesus: The Archaeological Evidence* (New York: HarperCollins, 2009).

Grant, Robert M. *A Historical Introduction to the New Testament* (New York: Harper and Row, 1963) 95, 102, 109, 121. Available online at NTSLibrary.com.

Heard, R.G. "The Old Gospel Prologues," *Journal of Theological Studies* 6 (1955) 7–9.

Hume, David. *An Enquiry Concerning Human Understanding* (1748), Section X, "Of Miracles."

Lessing, Gotthold Ephraim. "On the Proof of the Spirit and the Power" (1777).

Kane, J. P. "The Ossuary Inscriptions of Jerusalem," *Journal of Semitic Studies* (1978) 23 (2) 268–282.

Koester, Helmut. *Ancient Christian Gospels: Their History and Development* (Harrisburg, PA: Trinity Press, 1990) 35–37.

Mitchell, Margaret M. "Mark, the Long-Form Pauline Εὐαγγέλιον." *Modern and Ancient Literary Criticism of the Gospels: Continuing the Debate on Gospel Genre(s)*, Eds. R. M. Calhoun, D. P. Moessner, and T. Nicklas, WUNT, n.d., (2020) 201–218.

Theissen, Gerd and Merz, Annette. *The Historical Jesus: A Comprehensive Guide* (Minneapolis, MN: Fortress, 1996) 458.

Wilken. Robert L. *The Christians as the Romans Saw Them* (New Haven, CT: Yale University Press, 2003) 81.

Winn, Adam. *The Purpose of Mark's Gospel: An Early Christian Response to Roman Imperial Propaganda* (Tubingen: Mohr Siebeck, 2008) 157–167.

Witherington, Ben III. *Jesus the Sage: The Pilgrimage of Wisdom* (Minneapolis: Augsburg Fortress, 1994).